Fire in My Heart

Keys to Living a Life of Love and Prayer

Ann Shields

Servant Publications
Ann Arbor, Michigan

Published by Servant Books
P.O. Box 8617
Ann Arbor, Michigan 48107

Cover design and photograph by Michael Andaloro

Printed in the United States of America
ISBN 0-89283-385-8

91 92 10 9 8 7 6 5 4 3 2

Library of Congress Cataloging-in-Publication Data

Shields, Ann Therese.
  Fire in my heart : keys to living a life of love and
prayer / by Ann Shields
     p. cm.
  ISBN 0-89283-385-8
  1. Christian life—1960-. 2. Love—Religious aspects-
Christianity. 3. Prayer. 4. Shields, Ann Therese. I. Title.
BV4501.2.S4386   1988
248.4—dc19   88-11437
                                          CIP

Dedication

*In honor of my beloved parents who have
so generously given me to
the Lord and to his service*

Contents

Part I

A Life of Love

ONE

The Transforming Power of Love

T HE SHADOWS WERE LONG and the sky a dark orange as the
sun slowly edged down below the tops of the hills. Only a
few cars now rolled along the two-lane highway high atop the
steep bank of the river, and even fewer boats inched their way
around the gentle curve downstream from the town.

It had been different earlier, of course. During the day both
roadway and waterway had been alive with traffic, barges, and
trucks hauling their loads to and from the city. But now it was
evening, and evening meant a gradual ceasing of the day's
activity.

The man in the small wooden shed leaned back in his chair,
stretching arms and legs and back to shake off the effects of
having sat so long, reading the tattered paperback book. He
checked his pocket watch. Only a little while now until the last
train of the day would roll through. Then his work day would
be over, and he could go home.

The shed, perched atop the steep river bank, was his lonely
workplace. From here he could see the railroad tracks as they
wound their way through the hills, then across the river and on
into town.

Getting the trains safely across the river was the man's job.
From his wooden shed he controlled the rickety old turntable
bridge that controlled all the traffic up and down along the

11

river. Most of the time the bridge was turned so as to run parallel to the river. That way, the river was open for the various boats and barges to pass freely, and the cars on the highway could move freely through the railroad crossing.

But when a train was coming through, everything changed. Then the man would engage the big motors underneath the bridge, which would rotate until it linked up with the tracks on either side of the river. The man would lock the bridge into place and the train could cross the river safely, while the boats on the river and the cars on the highway waited.

It was, all in all, an extremely routine job. Sometimes the man's little boy would come by the shed in the afternoon. For a while he would play around the shed and watch the big bridge turn, slowly and noisily, across the river and back again. Then he would grow bored and scamper back home. Most of the time, the man was all alone.

He was alone now, as evening fell. Soon the last train of the day would come through. Mostly freight trains used these tracks now. But twice each day passenger trains rolled through, carrying their riders to the bigger cities farther down the valley. The last train of the day was one of these. It wasn't as big as in earlier times, when railroad travel was much in fashion. But its passenger load was steady. There would be three or four cars, counting the diner, between the engine and the caboose. After crossing the river it might stop in town just long enough to drop off a rider or two before continuing on its way.

The man snapped the watch shut and slipped it back into his pocket, then reached over and tripped the switch that started the bridge motor. Far in the distance he could hear the whistle of the passenger train: his signal to begin swinging the bridge into position. He threw the rest of the switches. There was a low groaning noise as the bridge began its slow turning. He could feel the floor of the shed vibrate and then, after a few moments, the familiar jolt as the bridge swung into place. He heard the whistle again, closer this time: the train would be just a mile or so away now, making the last winding curves before it emerged from the hills and crossed the river.

It was then that a little red light on the control panel caught the man's attention. A flash of fear shot through him like an electric current. The light meant that the bridge's automatic locking mechanism had failed to engage. If the tracks on the turntable bridge were not perfectly aligned with those on either side of the river—and if they were not properly locked in place—the train would jump the rails and plunge into the river below.

Fortunately, there was a manual locking mechanism that could be used when the automatic system failed. On each side of the bridge was a large steel lever. By setting the lever in the proper position, the bridge could be locked in place. The man bolted from the shed and toward the bridge junction on the near shore. It took all his strength to move the huge lever into place, securing the near end of the bridge.

Now the man hurried across the bridge to secure the junction on the far side. His heart was pounding as he grasped the lever in his hands and braced himself to pull it into place. The whistle sounded again, very close by. In just a few seconds the train would be upon him.

Just at that moment the man heard a sound that turned his blood to ice.

"Daddy! Daddy! Where are you?"

The child's voice came from the other side of the bridge by the wooden shed. His four-year-old son had come to watch the last train rumble across the bridge and then walk with his daddy back to the house for supper. Now he was on the tracks, stepping carefully from one railroad tie to the next, making his way out onto the bridge.

"Daddy? Where did you go?"

The man's first instinct was to cry out, "Run! Run!" But he realized immediately that there was not enough time. The tiny legs would not carry their owner fast enough. His next instinct was to race across the bridge himself, grab the boy and fling him to safety in the bushes along the far bank. But then, he knew, he could never get back in time to set the locking mechanism. The terrible choice was all too clear. If he left his post to rescue his child, the train filled with passengers would plunge into the river below. If he stayed, he could still save the train, but he could do nothing for the child. Either the passengers on the train must die, or his little boy must die. He could save one or the other, but not both.

In one horrible instant, he made his decision. Eyes blinded with tears, his hands gripped the lever. His legs and back strained as his powerful arms pulled the lever down, down, down into position.

The train rolled swiftly and safely across the river and on into the evening dusk. None of the passengers on board felt the train give even the slightest tremor as it hurled the tiny, broken body from the bridge. None of them saw the pitiful figure of the sobbing man, still bent over the cold steel lever long after the train had passed. None of them saw him, finally, draw himself up and walk slowly across the bridge toward home, there to search for the words to explain to his wife what had happened, and why.

For God So Loved the World

This is not, so far as I know, a true story. I tell it as it was told to me, as a sort of parable—a modern parable about God's love.*

The Bible has a great deal to say about God's love—both the love he has *for* us and the love he wants to pour *through* us to others.

The starting point is God's love for us. In the Gospel

---

*I do not know the origin of this story. I first read a version of it in a newsletter published by the Southern California Renewal Communities more than ten years ago.

according to John, we are told that "God so loved the world that he gave his only Son, that whoever believes in him should not perish but have eternal life" (Jn 3:16).

If you can comprehend the depth of what welled up in that trainman's heart to enable him to give up the life of his little son in order to save the lives of the men and women on the train—then you can just begin to understand the depth of love that God showed for you and me when he sent his beloved Son, Jesus Christ, to die for us.

God—the great God of heaven and earth—loved you and me so much that he sent his only Son to die so that we could live. God the Father gave what was most precious to him, gave what was dearest to him, gave what he loved the most: his Son. He gave all that he had when he gave us Jesus. He handed him over—handed *himself* over—to us, "knowing," in the words of one of my favorite songs, "we would bruise him, and smite him from the earth."

Why? Because he loved us. Because he loved us *that much*.

He loves you that much even now. Whoever you are, wherever you are, whatever you've done—as you read these words, God wants you to know that he loves you. There is no one outside his love. There is not one of us who can say, "Everyone else is loved, but not me. No one loves me." That's not true. God loves you at this very moment every bit as much as he did when he watched his Son die for you.

Because He Loved Us

Like his death, Jesus' whole life was a demonstration of God's love. Paul sums up the self-sacrificing character of Jesus' life in a moving passage from his letter to the Philippians:

Have this mind among yourselves, which is yours in Christ Jesus, who, though he was in the form of God, did not count equality with God a thing to be grasped, but emptied himself, taking the form of a servant, being born in the likeness of men. And being found in human form he humbled himself and became obedient unto death, even death on a cross. (Phil 2:5-8)

Jesus, the Son of God, was himself God, with all the powers and privileges and prerogatives of God. But Scripture says that he emptied himself of his godhead and took on the lowly nature of a human being, so that he could be one of us. Thus, as Scripture says, "For we have not a high priest who is unable to sympathize with our weaknesses, but one who in every respect has been tempted as we are, yet without sin" (Heb 4:15).

Being born in the likeness of men, he shared every experience that you and I are subject to. In perfect obedience to God, he shared our loneliness, our fear, our struggle, even our temptation. He took it all upon himself and carried it to Calvary, where he was obedient even to the point of suffering a cruel, humiliating death on the cross.

Why? Because he loved us. You and me. Because he wanted to open the way for us to return to the Father, from whom we were cut off because of our sin.

While We Were Still Sinners

And the truly phenomenal part—the part that always gives me pause—is that God did all this for us when we did not deserve it, did not understand it, could not even be grateful for it.

> While we were still weak, at the right time Christ died for the ungodly. Why, one will hardly die for a righteous man—though perhaps for a good man one will dare even to die. But God shows his love for us in that *while we were yet sinners* Christ died for us. (Rom 5:6-8)

For God to have given the life of his Son in exchange for our lives would have been astonishing enough had we been the kind of people who might be thought to deserve such treatment: had we been holy and righteous and virtuous in every way. But the fathomless depth of God's love is demonstrated, Paul says, precisely by the fact that he gave his Son for us when we could in no way be thought to deserve it: when we were still sinful and rebellious and ungrateful.

How foolish, then, is it for us to say, "God couldn't love me. Look at all I've done. Look how unworthy I am." It may well be true that we have done terrible things, and it is certainly true that we are hopelessly unworthy. Yet despite our sinfulness and our unworthiness, God gave up the life of his precious Son so that we might live.

Why? Because he loves us.

God so loved the world—so loved you and me—that he gave his Son. Knowing and clinging to that phenomenal truth is the foundation of all joy and peace and confidence in life. We must never let ourselves be robbed of the truth that God loves us. We need to hold it always in our hearts and minds.

A New Commandment

But the Bible does not stop with telling us of the love God shows to us. It also speaks of the love we are to show to one another.

> "A new commandment I give to you, that you love one another; even as I have loved you, that you also love one another. By this all men will know that you are my disciples, if you have love for one another." (Jn 13:34-35)

These are solemn words of Jesus to his followers: to you and to me no less than to those who were with him at the time. We are to love one another. To be precise, we are *commanded* to love one another. It is not merely a suggestion for making our lives happier (though it certainly produces that effect). It is a command.

And we are not to love others "just any old way." We are not to love them with merely human love. We are to love with divine love, with the love of Jesus himself. We are to love one another in the same way that Jesus loved us: by sacrificing ourselves, by laying down our lives for one another.

God's Love Flows Through Us

This is far more easily said than done. In fact most of us, the moment we do say it, immediately begin thinking of just how hard it *is* to put into practice. We think of the person who wronged us or spoke hurtfully to us. We think of the irritating habit in our spouse that drives us to distraction. We think of the utterly unlovable person who works across the aisle, or lives across the street. It would take a saint to love such people, and we are certainly not saints.

Unfortunately, that excuse is not available to us. Jesus did not say, "Those of you who are exceptionally holy, or who have unusual patience, are to love as I love." We are *all* commanded to love as he loved. That emphatically includes you and me.

Very well, then. We are commanded to do something we seem totally incapable of doing. Where does that leave us?

If we are wise, it leaves us relying on God. For just as surely as I know that God loves me, I know that he never commands me to do something without at the same time giving me what I need to accomplish it. He doesn't give us commandments and then leave us to figure out how to fulfill them. He *helps* us. He gives us his wisdom in Scripture to *teach* us how to love. He gives us the example of Jesus, to *show* us how to love. And he gives us his very own love, poured into our hearts, *with which* to love. Only as we receive his teaching, and follow his example, and let his love flow into us and through us, will we ever be able to love one another as he has loved us.

The Power of Love

Then we will begin to see amazing things. Because love has power. Power to transform people and situations. Love unifies what has been torn asunder. It brings hope where there has been despair. It brings confidence where there has been doubt. Love brings joy where there has been sorrow, life where there has been death.

I recently saw an example of the transforming power of love in an incident that happened to a friend of mine who works as a nurse. A new patient was brought to her ward, a man in his forties who had been diagnosed with AIDS. For some months he had been able to continue his normal life; then he was forced to leave his job and stay home most of the time; then he was confined to his bed: all in what should have been the prime of his life.

Now, at last, he had been brought to the hospital to die. He was bitter and fearful and frustrated, and he took out his feelings on everyone who came in contact with him—including my friend, who came into contact with him several times a day. Indeed, he seemed for some reason to reserve an extra portion of anger for her. He spat in her face when she leaned over to adjust his pillow. He swore at her continually. He even struck her on occasion.

How did she react? At first, she reacted the way most of us would. She felt hurt and angry. She wanted to retaliate—or at least to run away. But she didn't. She stayed, and she prayed.

"I didn't know what else to do," she told me later. "Nothing that I was doing as a nurse was making any difference. So I just prayed for him, and prayed, and prayed, and prayed."

For a while, it seemed that things only got worse. The man grew, if anything, more angry, more bitter, more hostile. By now he was taking it all out on his family. He completely alienated them. Even though he was dying, they wanted nothing to do with him, wanted never to see him again.

My friend continued to pray.

Then, about three days before the man died, his wife unexpectedly showed up in his room. For some reason, his usual reaction of rage and hostility didn't occur. There seemed to be something in her manner that calmed it.

What she had to say was very short and very simple.

"I've found Jesus," she told her husband, "and I want you to know that I forgive you and I want to ask you to forgive me."

The man began to weep. He reached out and embraced his wife, and the two of them wept together for a long time. A couple of days later, that wife was able to lead her husband to Christ. He repented of his sins and surrendered his life to God.

Why? Because of the love of God, channeled to him through the prayer of my nurse friend and through the faithfulness and obedience of his wife.

The Stinginess of Human Love

That story always helps me remember how important it is to love, and to keep on loving, and to call on God for help when it gets hard to love. It's a lesson I need to repeat often.

I will never forget the day I was shopping downtown and saw up ahead of me on the sidewalk an elderly man holding a white cane. He was standing at the edge of the curb, looking as though he wanted to cross the street.

I am embarrassed to confess that my first thought was, "It's a fake. He's not really blind. He's just using that cane to trick people. If I go to help him, he'll hit me with it and snatch my purse."

So there I stood, eyeing this poor man and thinking these terrible thoughts, when up walked this young woman. She stepped right in front of me and said gently to the man, "Sir, could I help you cross the street?"

I could see the tears in his eyes as he turned toward her. "Thank you," he said. "I didn't know how I was going to get to the other side."

By then I could feel the tears welling up in my own eyes. I was so ashamed of myself, at my selfishness and suspicion and fearfulness. Most of all I was ashamed at the stinginess of my love. After all that God had done for me! Now he had brought into my path such a beautiful opportunity to pass that love along to another, and I had failed.

"We Will Be Judged on Love"

Jesus says, "Love one another as I have loved you." You and I have available to us the power to transform our families, our work situations, our relationships. The power to do it is in the love of God that is poured out for us so that it may be poured through us to others. We are called by God to live a life of love. The only way we can do this is to stay close to him, to call on him every day for his grace and power in our lives. That means, as we shall see later, that we must live a life of prayer. As my nurse friend learned through her experience with that bitter, angry patient, prayer is the means by which we take in the love of God, as well as the means by which we channel it to others.

A life of love. A life of prayer. And a life of *faithfulness*. It was my unfaithfulness that choked off the love of God in my encounter with the blind man. By contrast, it was her faithfulness that enabled my friend to keep on praying for her difficult patient with such wonderful results.

A holy man known as John of the Cross once said, "In the twilight of our life, we will be judged on love." We will not be judged on our gifts, our talents, our achievements. We will not be judged on how hard we have worked or how much we have accomplished. We will be judged on how much and how well we have loved, on whether we have loved one another as Jesus loved us.

TWO

The Gift of Love

T HE STORY IS TOLD OF an American Indian tribe whose customs included a challenging rite of passage for its young men. They were considered children until age twelve, at which time they were expected to graduate to manhood. All their early training and instruction was aimed at preparing them for the day when they would leave childhood behind forever and become men.

The whole process culminated in a single night of ceremony and testing, after which they were accepted as braves of the tribe. The ceremony itself was awe-inspiring: the elders of the tribe, surrounded by all the rest of the men, were seated in solemn assembly to usher the young men into adulthood. The fires, the drums, the dancing, the ritual. Most of all, the anticipation of the ordeal to come and the question pounding away deep inside each boy's heart: *Am I good enough? Will I make it?*

Finally the rituals were completed and the time came for the climactic test. Each young boy was led away into the darkness with nothing but a knife and the clothes on his back to spend the night in the deep of the forest, all alone.

Let's focus on the experience of just one of these young boys. Like all the others, he had strained and agonized through the years of stern instruction and training. He had sat mesmerized before the fire that evening, watching the men of the tribe perform the rituals so old and familiar to them but so strange and new to him, who had never before been permitted to witness them.

Now he stood alone, in the deep darkness of the woods, clutching his hunting knife in his hand and listening to the pounding of his heart that seemed to drown out the familiar noises of the night.

No doubt you yourself know what it is like to be left all alone in a dark and strange place. Shapes take on weird, wild proportions in the moonlight. Noises seem magnified and ominous. Your imagination runs away with the slightest disturbance, creating visions of danger.

He could not possibly sleep. The shapes and sounds were too ominous, the possibilities of danger too frightening, the consequences of failing to endure the test too humiliating even to contemplate. He groped his way to a large, sturdy tree. Knife still clutched tightly in hand, he stood with his back to the tree so that he would have to defend himself in only three directions. There he planted himself, watching the shapes and shadows and listening to the sounds of the dark night.

After what seemed like half a lifetime had passed, the boy noticed that the darkness was starting to melt away. Soon one side of the sky was growing lighter, and in the rosy hues of sunrise he could begin to see his surroundings more clearly. Rocks and trees and bushes that had frightened him during the night began to take back their normal proportions and become themselves again. Now his heart began to pound even harder, not with fear this time but with jubilation mixed with inexpressible relief. It was over. He had made it.

For the first time in hours, he felt his muscles begin to relax and his breathing return to normal. With the coming of the sun he was free to return to the village.

He had taken only a few steps from the tree that had been his protector through the long night when he heard the snapping of a twig a few yards behind him. His heart leapt to his throat as he wheeled around and raised his knife to the ready. There, atop a large rock just behind the tree, silhouetted against the morning sky, stood a man. He was dressed in warrior's garb and he held a bow and arrow trained on the boy's chest. Slowly, slowly, he lowered the bow to his side, slipped down the back side of the rock, and stole away into the forest.

The boy stood silently, catching his breath. He understood instantly what had happened. Had the warrior wished to remain unseen and unheard, he could easily have done so. But he had made the small noise on purpose, had *meant* for the boy to see him. And he had meant for the boy to recognize him. As the warrior had lowered his bow to his side, just before he turned and disappeared into the woods, the boy had caught a glimpse of his face. It was his father. He had been standing there, watching over him all night, ready to spring to his rescue if needed. His father had been there all along.

God Is Always with Us

The first time I heard that story I thought to myself, "That's exactly how it is with us and our heavenly Father. He allows us to go through many trials and hardships, many fearful moments. He wants us to be brave, to stand firm, to endure, even to fight if need be, because he wants us to grow from childhood to spiritual maturity. But he is always there, watching over us, ready to come to our aid."

Isn't that how God the Father loved his own Son, Jesus? He allowed him to suffer trial and temptation, agonizing hardship, and even death. And yet he was always with him.

And he is always with us. No matter how trying our own circumstances might be, no matter how fearful, no matter how long and dark the night through which we must pass, our God is always with us. His love is always there for us.

God's Love Is for Each of Us

I emphasize this because I know how easy it is to hear those words, "God loves you," and let them roll off because they are so familiar. *Yes, yes. God loves me. How nice. So what else is new?*

But the truth that God loves us is not just a nice pious-sounding cliché that we pay lip-service to. We cannot just let it roll off our backs. We need to let the truth of God's love for us sink into the very core of our being, to take root deep within us, until it becomes the bedrock, the foundation of our lives.

Jesus told a story that shows what a difference it makes to build our lives on a firm foundation:

> "Every one then who hears these words of mine and does them will be like a wise man who built his house upon the rock; and the rain fell, and the floods came, and the winds blew and beat upon that house, but it did not fall, because it had been founded on the rock. And every one who hears these words of mine and does not do them will be like a foolish man who built his house upon the sand; and the rain fell, and the floods came, and the winds blew and beat against that house, and it fell; and great was the fall of it." (Mt 7:24-27)

Jesus compares what is built on rock to what is built on sand. What is built on rock is a life founded on the words of Jesus and on the assurance they bring us that God loves us. The foundation of our life must be the solid, firm assurance that we are so deeply, radically, totally loved by God that nothing that comes our way can undo us. Because even the house built upon the rock, Jesus' story indicates, will be buffeted by the winds and rain. In other words, every life will contain its share of difficulty and heartache. But when we rest secure in God's love for us, none of that can destroy us. None of it can shake our joy, our peace, our confidence.

God's Love Pierces the Darkness

Many years ago I went through a period of great personal anguish and difficulty. I especially remember one particular afternoon when I was about as low as low can be.

My surroundings at the time were not especially helpful: I was standing at the window on a gray, rainy afternoon, looking out at some rather bleak scenery. I was living in a mining town that had fallen on hard times, and all I could see from my window were slag heaps and empty railroad yards. The dismal view pretty well reflected my gloomy mood.

"O God," I prayed, "if you're there, if you care about me at all, help me. Do something to show me that you haven't abandoned me." I can't say I prayed that prayer with much hope. I don't think I really expected an answer. But as I turned away from the window, I felt as though I bumped into someone. I didn't, of course, at least not physically. There was no one there. Or was there?

Then I heard the voice of God, speaking directly to my heart. "Don't you know I've been with you all the time?" That was all he said. But in that moment, I felt the way I think our young Indian brave must have felt when he turned around and saw his father perched on that rock, watching over him. *Don't you know I've been with you all the time?* And in that moment, I *did* know. I knew, deep in my heart, that no matter how bleak things might be, my Father loved me and was always there for me.

God's Love Is Faithful

God's love for us is a faithful love. We read in the book of Isaiah the prophet:

> "For the mountains may depart
>   and the hills be removed,
> but my steadfast love shall not depart from you,
>   and my covenant of peace shall not be removed,
>   says the LORD, who has compassion on you."
>   (Is 54:10)

When we can look around us and see, figuratively speaking, how the mountains and hills are being shaken, it takes a real exercise of faith on our part to rest in the assurance of God's faithful, reliable, trustworthy love. We see the trying circumstances around us so clearly. We may see difficulties in the lives of our children, our spouse, our friends, our relatives. We say, "Why did this have to happen?" It takes faith to be able to say, "My God is in charge, and my God is a God of love."

But that is what we need to say. That is the truth that we must proclaim to ourselves, over and over and over. "God, I'm going to remember that you are a God of faithful love. I'm not going to harden my heart because of what has happened. I'm not going to close myself off from you. I'm going to remind myself that you love me and that you will never leave me. I'm going to put my faith in that fact and trust you to reveal your love and care to me in due time."

That, after all, was what Jesus did in the crisis of his life: he trusted in God's faithful love for him. When he had been mocked and scourged and stripped and spat upon and hung on the cross, did it look at that moment as though God the Father loved him? And yet he did. God loved him and never left him. He was with him all the time. And because Jesus put his faith in God's faithful love for him and endured the agony of the cross, God was able to raise him up from death and release through him the resurrection power that transforms you and me.

God's Love Conquers Sin

One Saturday afternoon I went to confess my sins and receive the Sacrament of Reconciliation. It was no different from any other Saturday afternoon, and as far as I was concerned, it was no different from any other time of confession and reconciliation. I walked into the confessional, sat down, and began the familiar rite. "Bless me, Father, for I have sinned. It has been two months since my last confession. I have committed the following sins." And then I rattled off a number of things I had done. It was a fairly unexciting list. I hadn't killed anybody or robbed any banks. Pretty tame stuff, all in all.

When I finished my little recitation, I sat back and waited for the priest to continue with the rite. But he didn't say anything. There was just silence. I waited. After a few moments he asked me, "Is there anything else?"

"No," I said. "That's about it." I wondered if I should feel embarrassed for taking up his time with such a penny-ante collection of sins.

Another long pause. What on earth was he doing? Maybe he was praying for me. But what for? Finally he breathed a deep sigh. "Let me ask you something," he finally said. "Are you *sorry* for anything you've confessed just now?"

Was I *sorry*? Why, *certainly* I was sorry. Not that I had done anything to be all that terribly sorry about, but... well, I was in confession, wasn't I? Sure, I was sorry. How could he ask such a question?

I arched my back and drew myself up to my full five-feet-three-inches and started to say, "Yes, Father, of course I'm sorry." But the words wouldn't come out. I began to think about what it really means to be sorry for my sin. I thought, "If I were really sorry, would I come back time after time repeating *all* the same sins? No. If I were truly sorry there would be some difference over time."

"No, Father," I finally whispered. "I guess I'm not really sorry for anything I've said."

He sat there quietly for a few moments before speaking. "I could grant you absolution," he said. "But I'd rather not."

I just stared at him. I had never had a priest say anything like that to me before—and there were times when I had confessed sins more serious than these.

"I mean, I *will* grant you absolution if you want me to," he went on. "There's nothing to say that I can't. All the conditions for the sacrament are fulfilled, technically speaking. But I'd rather not. I'd rather wait and have you come back when you have known sorrow for your sins."

I felt pretty small walking out of that confessional. But I had to admit that the priest's suggestion was a good one. I was troubled by my lack of remorse, too.

God's Love Is Merciful

For the next four months—yes, that's how long it took—I knelt before the Lord and asked for his help. "Lord, have mercy on me. You are the creator and I am the creature, and I have sinned against you. Break down the hardness of my heart so that I can know sorrow for my sins. Have mercy on me, that I might know how much I *need* your mercy."

And that is exactly what he did. He showed me who I was in relation to him. He showed me how my sin brought grief to him. He broke the hardness of my heart and led me to true sorrow for my wrong thoughts and words and actions. And then, out of that brokenness and humility, he brought me to a certainty of his forgiveness, of his merciful love for me. The Lord had mercy on me.

God's love is merciful. The book of Sirach says it so beautifully:

> You who fear the LORD, wait for his mercy,
>   turn not away lest you fall.
> You who fear the LORD, trust him,
>   and your reward will not be lost.
> You who fear the LORD, hope for good things,
>   for lasting joy and mercy.
> Study the generations long past and understand;
>   has anyone hoped in the LORD, and been
>   disappointed?
> Has anyone persevered in his fear and been forsaken?
>   has anyone called upon him and been rebuffed?
> Compassionate and merciful is the LORD;
>   he forgives sins, he saves in time of trouble.
>   Sir 2:7-11 (NAB)

Later in the same passage, the writer concludes, "Equal to his majesty is the mercy that he shows" (Sir 2:18). We so often think of the awesomeness, the power, the grandeur of God.

Well, equal to that majesty is the mercy that he shows to you and me. Receive that merciful love. Take it in. Absorb it. Don't try to reason it out. Don't try to earn it. You can't. You will never be worthy of it. But it is there for you. Be humble. Accept it and begin to lead a life befitting repentance.

God's Love Conquers Fear

The one person who, more than almost any other, encouraged me in my walk with the Lord was a friend of mine, a Sister of Mercy named Sister Baptista. Those of us who knew her well called her Bappy for short. She was many years older than I, but I thought of her as a friend. She was a woman of great holiness and courage and love. Sadly, she was also a woman who suffered from a seriously diseased heart. And I knew that despite her courage, she was afraid of dying.

For several years we prayed that God would heal her heart and prolong her life. But in time it became clear that that was not God's plan, but that he intended to bring her to himself. It was clear to her, too, and she tried to accept it peacefully. "I'm trying," she would say. "I'm trying. But I'm so afraid."

All this time she would speak to others about the faithful and merciful love of God. We would say to her, "Bappy, what about *you*? Don't you believe God loves you?" And she would answer, "Yes, of course I do. But there is still a part of me that is so afraid."

The day she was taken to the hospital I reached there as quickly as I could so that I could be by her side. Her situation was grave. But when I entered the intensive care room, I was overwhelmed with a sense of peace. I couldn't describe it, but it was there.

I started to say something to her, but quickly realized that she hadn't the energy to concentrate on conversation. So I just knelt down by her bedside, with my lips close to her ear, and began to pray the Twenty-third Psalm. *The Lord is my shepherd . . .*

She lay there, not moving, not showing any expression on

her face, until I reached the end of the psalm. *And I shall dwell in the house of the Lord all the days of my life.* Suddenly a faint smile played across her lips, and she repeated very quietly, "All the days of my life. All the days of my life."

Not wanting to tire her, I rose to leave. But before I did I heard her call to me. I turned around. She looked at me now with a huge smile on her face, and said simply, "We love you."

"Bappy, what do you mean?" I asked her. I wasn't sure what she meant by "we."

"Oh, child," she said, "Jesus and I, we love you." As she lay at the very gates of death, she felt such union with the Lord that she could say, "*We* love you."

God's Love Is Healing

She was healed. There was no fear, no anxiety. In the face of the one thing that had always terrified her, she could love. She could reach out and give me immeasurable comfort through her words. She could care for another, and not worry about herself. The faithful, merciful love of God had enveloped her and healed her of her fear.

That is the kind of healing love that God the Father has for you and me. I have witnessed dramatic physical healings. I have witnessed tremendous emotional and psychological healings. God's love provides those as well. But what I saw in my friend that night in the hospital was the greatest healing of all. That night I saw the love of God manifest as faithful, as merciful, as healing, and it spoke to me as nothing else before or since has spoken to me.

Let it speak to you, too. Let God's love come into your heart. Do you know God as faithful? As merciful? As the great healer? That is how he wants to make himself known to you. Open your heart to him. It's so easy to close ourselves off, to say, "Well, it's true for others but not for me." Or to say, "Poor me. I've been through so much. I have a right to be bitter." And all the while God stands so close to us, reaching out to us, waiting for us to reach out to him.

God's Love Is a Gift

He waits to give us his love, his faithful, merciful, healing love. And he offers it as a gift. Not as something we have to earn. As a gift. If you've never received it, I urge you to open your heart right now and to say to God simply, "I accept your gift. I accept your love in my life." That simple act of faith makes all the difference.

If you *have* received the gift of God's love before, I urge you to open your heart even wider and receive even more. God wants you to know his love ever more deeply. As you do, you are transformed, and God's kingdom comes forth. And as God's kingdom comes forth, we can all rise together as the people of God, who know who he is, who know his faithfulness, his mercy, his healing, his love.

THREE

Relying on God's Love

LIKE SO MANY OTHERS, I remember watching on television several years ago as the American hostages came home from their months-long captivity in Iran.

I could not help but wonder whether they were confused and even a bit overwhelmed by all the attention being paid to them. After all, these people had been living in a different world for more than a year. They were almost completely cut off from all contact with their homeland. All they knew was what they experienced around them day-to-day.

They might have hoped—but they could not have known for certain—that there were people back in America who knew of their plight and were working to rescue them. They had no way of knowing about all the hours spent by government officials and diplomats trying to free them. They could not read all the newspaper stories and magazine articles written about them or see any of the hours of television time devoted to them. They may well have been unaware of the dramatic military rescue attempt that failed so tragically.

And now, I thought as I watched them step down from the plane at the airstrip near Washington, D.C., here they are: surrounded by jubilant crowds and blaring brass bands and shouting reporters and glaring television lights, soon to be whisked away to the White House and be welcomed home on national television by the President of the United States. Did they ever in their wildest dreams, imagine that their ordeal would end this way? That there would be this kind of reception awaiting them when it finally did end?

The Reception that Awaits Us

I wonder whether we realize that the reception awaiting those hostages, glorious as it was, is but a pale glimmer of the reception that awaits you and me in heaven?

Like those hostages, you and I are foreigners living in captivity in a strange land. Our true home is in heaven with God our Father and Jesus our brother and the Holy Spirit. But we have our time to complete here, on earth, before we are released and returned to our homeland.

Like the hostages, we *feel* the separation. We feel almost totally cut off from our home, so surrounded are we by the circumstances of our day-to-day life. We hope—but sometimes we do not feel we know with certainty—that there is someone who knows of our plight, who is thinking of us, working on our behalf, trying to help us.

Little do we realize how much effort is being expended on our behalf to bring us safely home! Little do we realize how readily available to us is God's Holy Spirit. Little do we realize how deeply the Father is longing to draw us to himself, or how vigorously Jesus, who "always lives to make intercession for us," is praying for us at every moment of our lives (see Heb 7:25).

Little do we anticipate what a reception awaits us upon our arrival: angels and archangels, saints and martyrs, the "great cloud of witnesses" gathered there before the throne, cheering for *us* as we are brought into the presence of God. That is what lies ahead of us; that is what we have to look forward to.

If only we could see it and hear it and feel it *now*. What a difference it would make in our lives to know—to really and truly *know*—all that awaits us, all that is there for us now, in God's plan.

Well, we *can* know. God has made it known to us, and his Holy Spirit can bring it to our remembrance and make it real to us in our down-to-earth, day-to-day life experience. That is what happens to us as we come to know and understand and live in the love of God.

All this is part of what I call *a life of love*. A life of love is one lived in continual *awareness* of God's love. A life of love is one lived in continual *reliance* on God's love. And a life of love is one lived in continual *giving* of God's love to others. In this chapter I'd like to review some of what we've learned about the awareness of God's love, and then take a closer look at what it means to rely on God's love. Love for others is such an important topic that it will require a chapter in itself.

Embraced by God's Love

Jesus made many remarkable statements. Some of the most remarkable are recorded in the Gospel of John, particularly in the late chapters where John recounts some of the things Jesus told his closest disciples in what he knew were his last hours on earth.

One of the things he talked about was his and the Father's love for them. In chapter 15 we read: "As the Father has loved me, so have I loved you; abide in my love" (Jn 15:9). And a bit later, in chapter 17, Jesus prays to the Father for unity among his followers as a sign to the world:

> "The glory which thou hast given me I have given to them, that they may be one even as we are one, I in them and thou in me, that they may become perfectly one, so that the world may know that thou hast sent me and hast loved them even as thou hast loved me." (Jn 17:22-23)

Reflect for just a moment on what is revealed here. Jesus says that he loves us in just the same manner and degree as his

Father has loved him. Then he says that the Father, too, loves us just as much as he loves Jesus.

Now, surely the love that God has for his Son is the ultimate love. And yet Jesus tells us that it is with precisely this love that both he and the Father love us. To put it another way, the love that the Father and the Son (and, we can surely assume, the Spirit) have for one another is the very love into which you and I are embraced.

That is how much God loves each of us. It does not matter what we have done or what our circumstances are or what difficulties we face. The truth of Scripture does not change. We do not have a second-class love. We have the all-perfect love of the Father for the Son, and of the Son for the Father. That is our heritage.

Forgiveness: The Forgetfulness of God

Out of that love, as we have seen, flows forgiveness. Forgiveness of *all* our sin. I remember a time, several years ago, when I was praying; for some reason I kept remembering a number of things I had done wrong over the years. I kept saying to the Lord, "I'm sorry, Lord. I'm sorry, Lord." And it was as though I heard him say, "For what?" So I recounted some of my past sins that were troubling me. And I heard the Lord say, "I don't recall anything like that."

It was then that I remembered what God had said through the prophet Isaiah: "I, I am He who blots out your transgressions for my own sake, and I will not remember your sins" (Is 43:25).

In God's mind, to forgive is to forget. When we sin, of course, we need to repent, ask God to forgive us, and strive by his grace not to sin again in that area. But once we *have* repented of our sin and received God's forgiveness, we need no longer call it to mind and brood over it. God, having forgiven our sin, puts it out of his mind. That is how much he loves us.

The God Who Keeps Covenant

God's love, as we have seen, is faithful. It is solid, sure, unchanging. It is like rock that you can build on without fear, because you know it is going to be immovable.

God is the God who *keeps covenant*. A covenant is a solemn agreement. It is unlike a contract, in that with a contract, once one party has broken the agreement the other party is no longer bound by it. But with a covenant, each party remains bound by the agreement no matter what the other party does. God has made a covenant with us. No matter whether we keep our end of the bargain or not, he will keep his. "If we are faithless, he remains faithful—for he cannot deny himself" (2 Tm 2:13).

God's love is faithful. That is his nature. He will never leave us, abandon us, walk away from us. We will never turn to him only to hear him say, "Oh, I'm sorry. I have someone else to look after right now." He is faithful to us. That is how much he loves us.

There is no end to God's love. No limit. There is nothing he will not do for us out of love. He proved that when he sent his only Son to die for us. "He who did not spare his own Son but gave him up for us all, will he not also give us all things with him?" (Rom 8:32).

All things. Scripture says God will give us all things. Anything you can think of that is for our good, that is holy, that is pure—the God who loved us enough to give his Son for us will never hold it back from us.

"Why Do You Sell Me Short?"

We are loved that much, you and I. How clearly do we see it? How firmly do we hold on to it? How is it that we cling to the things of this world so tenaciously, as though we did not have a God who loved us and was ready to provide us with everything

we need? Why do we rely on so many things other than the love
of God?

Several months ago I was praying with a group of people and
one of the men in the group shared what he had sensed to be a
word from the Lord. He believed he had heard the Lord saying:

*Why do you sell me short? Why do you fail to call upon my name?
Look around you. See how the world is filled with men and women
who chase to and fro as if it were their effort that caused progress.
They worship their political processes. They worship the gods they
carry in their wallets. They worship their own talents and
achievements.*

*But it is not they who cause things to move ahead, says the Lord. It
is I. I am the Lord of heaven and earth. I am the one whose right
hand is extended in power. It is those who see what I am doing and
join themselves to me who move forward, says the Lord. It is those
who call upon my name and ask me to act who see change, who see
progress, who see spiritual opposition set aside.*

*How many times have I been ready to respond to you but you did
not call upon me? Instead you trusted in yourselves. How many
times have I seen you with your families, your marriages, your
finances, your jobs, your service to me—and in every way you are
struggling under your own strength and with your own wisdom.
I was ready to respond to you but you did not call upon me.*

*Why do you sell me short? Call upon my name and see the power of
my Holy Spirit at work in your life and in the world.*

What Do We Rely On?

In what ways might these words apply to you? What is it that
you are relying on, other than the love of God?

Material possessions? There is nothing wrong with them in
themselves. If God gives them to you, fine. Thank him for them
and use them for his glory. But do not rely on them for security
or happiness.

Other people? How often we find ourselves saying, "If I could just get into that circle . . ." "If I could just be married to that man or that woman . . ." "If I could just have that person for a friend . . ." Now, God wants us to have good relationships with others. This is one of his greatest blessings. But they are not to be the *foundation* of our life.

Gifts and abilities? These are wonderful, and praise be to God for lavishing his gifts upon us and equipping us to serve him so marvelously. But we cannot rely on our gifts and abilities to bring us what only God can truly bring us.

What else is there that we are tempted to rely on? Our job? Our marriage? Our health? Sometimes we even come to rely on sinful patterns of behaving and relating that enable us to control or dominate others: harsh speech, gossip, sexual habits, anger, bitterness, and the like.

So many things clamor for our attention. So many things tempt us to draw our eyes away from God, to place our trust in something other than him and his love for us. It afflicts all of us, in one way or another, to one degree or another. And yet look at who God is for us. Look at the ways he has blessed us. Look at the ways he wants to bless us.

Under God's Reign

Once when I was praying I got a picture in my mind of a waterfall, a huge, mighty waterfall. And far off to one side, perched on an outcropping of rock, tiny alongside the greatness of the waterfall, was me. I was well out of reach of the crashing, tumbling water. In fact, where I was standing I could just be reached by the mist that rose up from the waterfall.

"That's the way you relate to living in my love," the Lord said to me. "You stand carefully off to one side, close enough to be touched by the mist but never really diving in. You're busy serving me, but you don't fully rely on me. Come closer. Draw nearer. Let yourself surrender to my love. Be drenched in it."

It reminded me of something someone had shared during a prayer session a few weeks before. The person had sensed the Lord saying to us:

> *I reign over the heavens and I reign over the earth. I reign over nations and I reign over rulers. I reign over the events that unfold in the world. I reign over all these things without invitation and without commission for I am the creator and the ruler of all.*
>
> *But I want to reign over your hearts and over your lives and for this I await your invitation. If there is any area of your life that is not yet under my reign, invite me in. If there is any area of your life in which you have needs, or in which darkness reigns, invite my reign of life and light and love to come in. I ask you to invite me, for it is out of my love for you that I long to reign over your heart, over every area of your life.*

Surrender to God's Love

I believe that is God's attitude toward every one of us. He loves us so much that he longs to reign over every facet of our existence. And like me in the picture of the waterfall, we stand off to the side, just getting the mist from the waterfall. Or worse: we run away, run after other things, looking elsewhere for peace and security and hope.

But peace and security and hope are to be found nowhere else. They lie in the heart of God. Nothing we seek, nothing we desire, nothing we hope for can compare with the love of God. I believe God may want to speak to you even now as you read these words: "Let go. Whatever you are clinging to, let it go. Set it aside, and surrender yourself to me, so that you might experience my power, my life, my love. Not just a mist, but a flood. Not just every now and then, but every moment of every day. Let go."

God Meets Our Needs

Amazing things happen when we surrender to God and decide to rely on his love. I know a man, a carpenter, who had been out of work for several months. His wife had serious back trouble and was confined to bed, leaving him to care for their small children. He got odd jobs whenever he could, but was unable to find steady employment. Meanwhile the family was forced to live on their savings, which slowly dwindled away until there was nothing left in the bank. The whole time, he and his wife prayed steadfastly: "Lord, we are your servants. We rely on you, on your love for us and our children. We know that you'll look after us."

One afternoon he was doing an odd job that had come up, replacing the paneling in a friend's house. The first part of the job was to tear out the old wall, which had been in place for a long time—since long before the present owner had bought the place. He ripped down a section of the old paneling, and a single dollar bill came fluttering out and landed at his feet.

He chuckled, set the bill down on a window ledge, and went back to work. He ripped out another section of the wall, and more bills came out—lots of them. As he continued, the money kept coming, until there was dust and plaster and dollar bills flying all over the room. He was pulling out money by the handful. By the time he was done, he had found more than $1500 stashed behind that old wall.

His friend, the owner of the house, was also a Christian. He knew the handiwork of God when he saw it and recognized immediately that this was God's way of meeting his friend's need. He insisted that he keep a good portion of the money. In a marvelous way, out of his great love, in response to prayer, and through the goodness of others, the Lord provided for the needs of his servant.

Bearing up under Hardship

It should come as no surprise that even those who rely on God's love have to endure hardship and difficulty, as my carpenter friend did for so many months. Scripture makes no secret of the fact that trials will be part of our lives as Christians. St. Paul was certainly one who knew how to rely on

God's love, and yet his descriptions of bearing up under hardship are among the most poignant to be found anywhere:

> For we do not want you to be ignorant, brethren, of the affliction we experienced in Asia; for we were so utterly, unbearably crushed that we despaired of life itself. Why, we felt that we had received the sentence of death; but that was to make us rely not on ourselves but on God who raises the dead; he delivered us from so deadly a peril, and he will deliver us; on him we have set our hope that he will deliver us again. (2 Cor 1:8-10)

God sometimes asks a great deal of us. But he never asks more of us than he is prepared to give in return. As he calls us to let go of the things we are relying on, as we let go of the things we are looking to for security and hope and peace, as we place our reliance on the Lord, he gives us security and hope and the peace that passes understanding.

Let Go!

That is our inheritance as sons and daughters of God. If we are not experiencing it, it is because we have not yet learned to trust in him, to open our hands and let go. Can you hear the Lord speaking to you, even now, calling you to surrender more to him, pointing out those things in your life that you need to turn over to him?

The Lord is there for you. He is eager to reign over more and more of your life, as you let go of even those things you are most afraid to let go of. He knows how important it is that we do let go. He knows what joy and peace is waiting for us when we do. He knows what heartache and pain we create for ourselves when we do not. He spoke of it in strong terms through his prophet, Jeremiah:

> Thus says the LORD:
> "Cursed is the man who trusts in man

and makes flesh his arm,
    whose heart turns away from the LORD.
He is like a shrub in the desert,
    and shall not see any good come.
He shall dwell in the parched places of the wilderness,
    in an uninhabited salt land.
Blessed is the man who trusts in the LORD,
    whose trust is the LORD.
He is like a tree planted by water,
    that sends out its roots by the stream,
and does not fear when heat comes,
    for its leaves remain green,
and is not anxious in the year of drought,
    for it does not cease to bear fruit."
                         (Jer 17:5-8)

Notice God says that heat and drought—that is, hardship and heartache—will come. He does not promise us a life free of suffering. But he does promise us his love, and his abiding presence in our lives. He does promise that if we rely on him and on his love, he will give us the strength we need for whatever comes our way. He promises his peace, which passes all understanding. He promises us the presence of the Holy Spirit with all his gifts: wisdom, understanding, counsel, fortitude, knowledge, piety, fear of the Lord. He promises us the great gifts of faith, hope, and love.

Do you want to receive all that God has for you? Then let go! Let go of what you are clinging to. You may be clinging to the kinds of things I described earlier in this chapter. You may be clinging to past hurts, to bitterness, to resentment—you may even feel *entitled* to cling to them.

But think of Jesus. He endured false accusation, mockery, and betrayal. He knew great pain as his followers left him right in the midst of his suffering. But he chose even then to trust his Father.

He was making a way for you. Let go of those things that cause hardness of heart. Decide to forgive those who have hurt you. Decide to rely on God's love, and you will see him act in your life. You will see him work in your marriage and in your family, in your work and in your relationships. You will see new strength, new hope, new confidence in your personal life. You will see the glory of God.

Don't sell the Lord short. Let go, and rely on God's love.

FOUR

The Father's Will

IT WAS ONE OF THOSE DREARY, drizzly days that force school teachers to cancel recesses and make school children grouchy. But even gloomy weather could not get me down today. I was eight years old and in the third grade. My mother had gone into the hospital that morning. "Today is the day!" my father had told me with a grin. "You're going to have a new baby brother or sister."

I had known about it for months, of course; months of endless questions about when the baby would finally arrive and what its name would be and where it would sleep and . . . But none of that really mattered now. All that mattered now was that I was going to have a new baby brother or sister. Daddy had said so.

Somehow I got through school that day without bursting from excitement and anticipation. When the last bell finally rang I bolted down the hallway and out the front door of the school, into the rainy afternoon. There on the street corner was my father. He was just standing there in the rain, hands in pockets, head uncovered, and as I got closer I could see tears mixed with the raindrops that ran down his cheeks. He was crying. All he said to me was, "You don't have a baby sister."

I was only eight years old, but I understood. I understood that my little sister had died. And I understood that there were some promises that were beyond my earthly father's ability to fulfill.

Promise of the Father

But our heavenly Father can fulfill every promise he has ever made to us. After he had risen from the dead, Jesus spoke to his disciples about one of the Father's most special promises:

> "Thus it is written, that the Christ should suffer and on the third day rise from the dead, and that repentance and forgiveness of sins should be preached in his name to all nations, beginning from Jerusalem. You are witnesses of these things. And behold, I send the promise of my Father upon you; but stay in the city, until you are clothed with power from on high." (Lk 24:46-49)

Jesus spoke again of the promise of the Father just before he ascended into heaven:

> And while staying with them he charged them not to depart from Jerusalem, but to wait for the promise of the Father, which, he said, "you heard from me, for John baptized with water, but before many days you shall be baptized with the Holy Spirit." (Acts 1:4-5)

The promise of the Father was that he would send his Spirit. And that Spirit would be for us a paraclete, a counselor, an advocate, a comforter. He would be the Spirit of truth. He would remain with us forever. He would empower us to do even greater works than Jesus had done.

We Are Never Alone

Have we not experienced the Holy Spirit guiding us, counseling us, comforting us? Leading us deeper and deeper into the truth? Empowering us to live for and serve the Lord? Standing by us in all circumstances?

I learned a powerful lesson about how the Holy Spirit stands by us during a trip to Australia thirteen years ago. We were hop-scotching our way across the Pacific Ocean, and had stopped briefly for refueling at one of the islands. We had only just taken off again when the pilot addressed us over the P.A. system.

"Ladies and gentlemen," he said in that calm, measured voice that all airline pilots seem to use when they have bad news, "we seem to be having a little, uh, *technical* difficulty with the aircraft. We're going to have to jettison our fuel and try to land back on Tahiti. Please follow the instructions of the flight attendants." The flight attendants then began preparing us for a crash landing.

I will never forget sitting there, looking out the window, watching thousands of gallons of fuel being dumped out, feeling the big, lumbering 747 begin its emergency descent. I confess I was nervous. I examined my conscience. Then I prayed the Lord's Prayer. As I did, I heard the Lord speak to my heart, just as clearly and plainly as though he had been seated right next to me: *I am the Father who loves you.*

Even in that fearful moment when I thought I might die, the Spirit was there reminding me of everything Jesus had taught, just as Jesus promised he would be (Jn 14:26). The promise of the Father is that through the Holy Spirit he will remain with us forever. We are never alone. Never. We need not give in to the lies of the evil one that we are alone, that we are isolated, that we have no one to stand by us. We are never alone. The Spirit is with us always. The Father keeps his promise. We can trust him.

"You Cared for Me Then"

We can trust him in seemingly small and insignificant ways, as well as in more dramatic ways. I learned something about this later during that same trip to Australia.

We were staying in a large downtown hotel that had a trash incinerator. On each floor was a chute that carried refuse from the upper floors to the basement. Somehow—I've never been quite sure how—our return plane tickets got put in that chute by the maid and dropped fourteen floors to the incinerator in the basement.

We went to the manager and told him what had happened. Our departure time was less than two hours away. Was there any way he could help us? "If your tickets have gone to the incinerator, I'm afraid there's nothing to be done," he told us. "You can go downstairs and talk to the engineer, but I really don't think there's any way to recover them." It did not look too promising, but there did not seem to be any alternative. Off we went to the basement.

We found the incinerator room quickly enough—all we had to do was walk toward the heat. We went into a room that made me think of the three young men in the fiery furnace described in the book of Daniel. The floor, walls, and ceiling were all brick; one entire wall was the door of the incinerator. When the engineer opened it, the chamber was so big I could have stepped in and walked around in it.

We explained our situation. Was there any way to look for our plane tickets?

"Well," he said, looking up toward the ceiling, "I haven't opened the chute since four o'clock yesterday afternoon, and it's two in the afternoon now, and you say you were on the fourteenth floor . . ."

It was pretty clear what he was trying to say. There was more than a day's worth of trash from the entire hotel backed up in that chute. What were the chances of finding our "needle" in a haystack that big?

The other people from the conference, who were there with me, caught the man's drift. "Come on," they said. "Let's go. This is no use."

But all I could think of was the way the Lord had spoken to me on the flight over, how he would always be with me and look after me. Feeling a bit foolish, I said to the engineer, "Couldn't we just give it a try?"

He rolled his eyes. "Okay, lady," he said. "If you really want to."

When he reached up and pulled the chain that opened the chute, a huge mound of trash came pouring down into the bed of the furnace. There was so much that it spilled out the doorway and into the room where we were standing. We were standing ankle-deep in it.

The engineer took a rake and began sifting through the huge mound of trash. As he raked, he stirred up the coals in the incinerator, and within about thirty seconds we found ourselves surrounded by flames that were three feet high. The people with me were getting very nervous now. "We should go," they said.

I just stood there, looking at the flames, thinking to myself, "Father, you promised to care for me."

Right then, two small packets of paper fluttered down from the chute overhead and came to rest on the ledge right next to me. I immediately thought, "They couldn't be airplane tickets." But they were. I then thought, "They couldn't be *our* airplane tickets." But they were! They weren't even singed. We grabbed those tickets, ran upstairs praising God all the way, leaving the engineer in the furnace room standing in open-mouthed astonishment.

Many times since then, when things are difficult, when circumstances seem to be against me, I think back to that incinerator in Australia and I say, "Father, you cared for me then and you're caring for me now. You're a faithful God. All your promises are true. I know I can trust you."

The Greatest Gift

The Holy Spirit dwells within us to enable us to live a life of love. It is the Spirit within us that enables us to experience God's love for us. It is also the Spirit within us that enables us to share God's love with others.

Jesus said that when the Holy Spirit came among us, we

would be able to do even greater works than he had done. Have we not begun to see them? Have we not seen people healed and delivered? The lame walk? The blind see? The deaf hear? And God has many more wonders yet to work in our midst.

But the greatest work of the Holy Spirit is not healing, or deliverance, or miracles. The greatest work of the Spirit is love. Jesus spoke strongly of those who miss this crucial point:

> "Not every one who says to me, 'Lord, Lord,' shall enter the kingdom of heaven, but he who does the will of my Father who is in heaven. On that day many will say to me, 'Lord, Lord, did we not prophesy in your name, and cast out demons in your name, and do many mighty works in your name?' And then will I declare to them, 'I never knew you; depart from me, you evildoers.'" (Mt 7:21-23)

Strong words! But they are there for our good, to point us to the one thing that Jesus desires from us above all else: that we do "the will of the Father."

And what is the will of the Father?

> And one of the scribes came up and heard them disputing with one another, and seeing that he answered them well, asked him, "Which commandment is the first of all?" Jesus answered, "The first is, 'Hear, O Israel: The Lord our God, the Lord is one; and you shall love the Lord your God with all your heart, and with all your soul, and with all your mind, and with all your strength.' The second is this, 'You shall love your neighbor as yourself.' There is no other commandment greater than these." (Mk 12:28-31)

The Will of the Father

The will of the Father is for us to love God with everything that is in us, and to love our neighbor as ourselves. The first part of this—the love that we have for God in response to the love he shows for us—we have discussed at length already. I'd like to talk more now about the second part—our love for one another.

Very few precepts are emphasized as strongly and as repeatedly in the New Testament as the importance of our love for one another. Jesus said:

"A new commandment I give to you, that you love one another; even as I have loved you, that you also love one another. By this all men will know that you are my disciples, if you have love for one another." (Jn 13:34-35)

In his first letter, the apostle John points out that a life of love must include love of neighbor as well as love of God. It is impossible, John says, to have one without the other:

Beloved, if God so loved us, we also ought to love one another. If any one says, "I love God," and hates his brother, he is a liar; for he who does not love his brother whom he has seen, cannot love God whom he has not seen. And this commandment we have from him, that he who loves God should love his brother also. (1 Jn 4:11, 20-21)

The apostle Paul likewise points out the futility of a Christian life lived without love for others:

If I speak in the tongues of men and of angels, but have not love, I am a noisy gong or a clanging cymbal. And if I have prophetic powers, and understand all mysteries and all knowledge, and if I have all faith, so as to remove mountains, but have not love, I am nothing. If I give away all I have, and if I deliver my body to be burned, but have not love, I gain nothing. (1 Cor 13:1-3)

If we are to take the Scripures at all seriously, if we are to heed Jesus' warning that we "do the will of the Father," then we are simply going to have to become serious about loving one another.

Five Principles for Loving One Another

Clear enough. But how do we actually *do* it? Loving other people is one of those things that is very easy to talk about but very difficult to do. I would like to share five simple principles that I have learned over the years about how we can love one another and love the Lord together in unity.

The first is, never ask *whether* you will work out a difficulty in a relationship, only ask *how*. I was part of a prayer group that made this resolution and it radically changed the way we related to one another. When we leave ourselves the option—"Maybe I'll try to straighten things out, maybe I won't"—we will too frequently take the option that leaves things unresolved. And unresolved relationship difficulties only get worse as time goes on.

The second is, hold no resentment. In his Second Letter to the Corinthians, Paul teaches us that we should "take every thought captive to obey Christ" (2 Cor 10:5). Sometimes we resolve a difficulty on the outer level but not on the inner level. That is, we go through the right motions and say the right words with the other person, but inside we still haven't released our bitterness. We've said the words, "I forgive you," with our mouths. But our hearts are saying, "Oh, no I don't." God will enable us to take every thought captive to Christ, so that we can put away bitterness and resentment.

The third principle: speak no evil. Probably most relationship breakdowns happen because of something that someone has said. James, in his Epistle, warns us that the tongue is "a restless evil, full of deadly poison" (Jas 3:8). That is why Paul urges us, "Let no evil talk come out of your mouths, but only such as is good for edifying, as fits the occasion, that it may impart grace to those who hear" (Eph 4:29).

It is a great challenge to live up to this teaching. I once lived with a group of people who decided we were going to take this teaching seriously, and we worked diligently at living it out. It was tough! One of the first things we discovered was how much of our table conversation consisted of analyzing and criticizing politicians and entertainment figures and sports stars whose often-unedifying private lives were glorified in newspapers and on television. When we got serious about not slandering (not "speaking against") others, it was remarkable how many conversations had to come to a screeching halt. But we stuck with it, learning how to avoid letting evil talk pass our lips.

Go the Extra Mile

The fourth principle is, never give up. Put away the attitude that says, "Well, I've done all that's reasonable for me to do. I can't do anything more. To heck with the whole thing." Scripture makes it clear that relationship difficulties among brothers and sisters in the Lord are serious matters that deserve going the extra mile to resolve.

A friend of mine, a magazine editor, once got into a mild dispute with an author whose manuscript he had mishandled. My friend was at fault, and both he and the author knew it. He wrote a letter to the author, apologizing for his error and asking forgiveness. To his surprise he received a rather sharp reply, to the effect of, "You're darn right it's all your fault," with no forgiveness extended. My friend tried again. This time there was simply no reply.

Now many of us, at this point, would give up trying to straighten things out, figuring, "Well, I've done all I can do." But my friend was unwilling to let it go at that. He wrote a third letter, asking if there was anything more he could do to make clear how sorry he was for what he had done wrong, and saying that he didn't want to let the matter rest until he and the author were reconciled.

That, finally, did the trick. The author responded with a

gracious note, forgiving my editor friend and apologizing for his own momentary hardness of heart.

The fifth principle sums up a theme that has been running through the previous ones: always take the initiative to resolve relationship problems. Two sayings of Jesus help to drive home this point:

> If your brother sins against you, go and tell him his fault, between you and him alone. If he listens to you, you have gained your brother. (Mt 18:15)
> If you are offering your gift at the altar, and there remember that your brother has something against you, leave your gift there before the altar and go; first be reconciled to your brother, and then come and offer your gift. (Mt 5:23-24)

Do you see the thread that runs through these two teachings? If you sin against your brother, *you go* and seek reconciliation. If your brother sins against you, *you go* and seek reconciliation. No matter whether it is he or you who causes the original problem, *you go* and initiate the process of reconciliation.

I once had an opportunity to put this teaching into practice in a remarkably literal way. I was in the midst of a rather serious disagreement with someone, and I was letting my pride and my anger get in the way of seeking a resolution. Then the Lord, in a masterpiece of strategic planning, thoughtfully arranged for the two of us to be at the same Mass one Sunday. We came to the Greeting of Peace, that part of the Mass in which we express our unity with one another. Suddenly the words of Matthew 5:23-24 came to mind: *If you are offering your gift at the altar. . .*

I knew what I had to do. I got up from my seat. The other person got up from her seat. We literally met each other halfway. That is what these two Scripture passages intend. If both parties know they have the responsibility to take the initiative, then they will meet each other on the way. How much easier it is to resolve difficulties when both parties approach it this way. In my situation, we embraced one another and prayed for the grace to resolve our problem peacefully. It really works!

A Life of Love, a Life of Freedom

One person who, it seems to me, epitomizes a life of love is Mother Teresa of Calcutta. She not only lives in constant awareness of and reliance upon God's love for her, but she constantly radiates that love to others.

I once had the opportunity to spend the day with her. It was a great privilege to see such a marvelous woman of God, who has given her all to serve the poorest of the poor, "up close and personal." At one point during the day I asked her, "Mother, what is it like when you travel to the West and you see all the wealth and the wastefulness? How does that affect you?"

"Well," she said, "when I am at a dinner and they pass a big platter of meat down the row, I can only think of the children who scramble for a single grain of rice under the table that someone may have dropped. But then..." she paused for just a moment, and then gave a little wave of her hand in front of her face, "but then I stop, because Jesus said, Do not judge, and so I do not judge."

That, I think, is why Mother Teresa is who she is, and why God can use her as he does. She is obedient to the word of God. She knows what Jesus said: "If you love me, you will keep my commandments" (Jn 14:15). And because she wants to live a life of love, she lives a life of obedience and freedom.

That freedom is not just for the Mother Teresas of the world. It is for you and me as well. It is for all God's little ones.

Many years ago, I came in contact with a thirteen-year-old girl who suffered enormously at the hands of her own parents. They were alcoholics. They were abusive to her. They threw her out of the house when she was very young and abandoned her to life on the streets. For several years she roamed the streets, encountering every kind of sin, evil, and perversion. Understandably, she was bitter toward her parents, who so thoroughly failed her. For years she went from one difficulty and crisis to another.

But because of constant prayer on her behalf by a few Christian friends who refused to give up, that young girl finally met the Lord and gave her life to him. And God blessed her, enabling her to get a General Equivalency Diploma and further training for a good job. Her police record was "wiped away" for crimes that she had committed as a juvenile. She had every chance to start life anew. But the greatest blessing God gave her, the blessing that made all the earthly opportunities possible, was a whole new life in Jesus Christ. He *changed her heart*. She said to me, "I have come to know that God really loves me and forgives me. He is my Savior. And I have come to love my parents. I forgive them. No matter what they have done to me, I love them."

Can you sense the power that produces that kind of love? It's the power that can renew the face of the earth, from the streets of Calcutta to the streets of Times Square to the street where you live. It's the power that can change lives, from Mother Teresa to my young friend to you and me.

That power—the power to live a life of love—is available to us. The question is, Will we respond to it? Will we accept it? Will we open our hearts wide to receive the faithful, merciful, healing love of God, to let it pour into us and pour out from us to all those around us? Will we decide to live a life of love, in the grace and power of the Holy Spirit?

Part II

A Life of Prayer

FIVE

The Joyful Duty

ONE OF THE HARDEST THINGS FOR ME to do is to remember all the little things that need to be done to keep a car in good running order. I have a fairly simple-minded philosophy about cars. If they start when I turn the key on, go when I step on the gas, and stop when I step on the brakes, then I am happy. I assume that everything is as it should be, and I just forget about it.

Sometimes, though, a car will fool you. It seems that you can ignore how much oil is in the engine and how much air is in the tires for a long time, yet the car will continue to run pretty well so that you assume everything is okay. Then, all at once, all kinds of problems develop. The car will not run right. Maybe it will not even start. Neglecting all those routine maintenance items has finally caught up with you. Now you are in for a big repair bill and a lot of inconvenience—all because you did not keep up with the basics.

Life with the Lord works in much the same way. As I have already said, a life of love is drawn from a life of prayer. The condition of our prayer life will often determine how well we will be able to receive God's love, and how well we will be able to give that love to others.

But our prayer life, like an automobile, has a number of basic elements that must be properly kept up if it is to keep running smoothly. We can neglect them for a while, and our life with the Lord may seem to keep moving along smoothly. But before long we run into trouble—we find ourselves feeling "out of touch" with God, unable to conquer temptation, unable to love others as we should—all because we did not keep up with the basics.

That is what I want to do in this chapter: review some of the basic elements that help us establish and maintain our prayer life.

The Ultimate Fulfillment

To begin with, I would like to share about an attitude that has helped me keep my prayer life in the proper orientation.

It is this: that prayer is a joyful duty.

Prayer began to take on a new dimension for me when I realized that it was not just something I did *when* I felt like it, *because* I felt like it. It was something I did because I was *supposed* to do it, because God *called* me to do it, because I was created to do it.

Prayer is what I was made for. God created me to know him, to love him, and to serve him. The most basic expression of the knowledge, love, and service of God is prayer. When I pray, I am reaching my ultimate fulfillment in this life.

So prayer is a duty. But it is a *joyful* duty, because it is the deepest expression of what I was created for and the richest source of God's blessing in my life.

Prayer for me is a sign of my commitment to the Lord. That commitment needs to go beyond mere words, or mere feelings. It needs to find actual, concrete expression. The most basic form of that expression is faithfulness to worship and prayer.

Imagine a mother who said, "Of course I'm committed to my children. But I don't feel like serving them today. I don't feel like cooking dinner or doing the laundry. I don't feel like sitting down with them and hearing about their day or giving them a hug and telling them I love them." Or imagine a father who said, "Sure, I'm committed to my family, but I just don't feel like going to work so that I can provide for them." We might wonder just how "committed" to their children such parents really were!

I have come to see that it is the same between God and me. I have surrendered my whole life to the Lord. I am committed to him. It does not make sense for me to say, "I don't feel like praying today, so I won't bother." That is not how commitment works. Prayer is a sign, an expression, of my commitment to God. I have a responsibility to come before him in prayer, regardless of my feelings on a particular day.

Prayer is a joyful duty. Seeing it that way has helped me grow in faithfulness in prayer, and as a result prayer has helped me grow in God's love.

Variety and Similarity

In talking about the elements of prayer, I am going to share the elements that are part of my own prayer life.

Now immediately I must point out that no two persons' lives are going to be exactly alike, nor are any two persons' *prayer* lives going to be exactly alike. I am a woman, living a special commitment to remain single for the Lord, as part of a sisterhood of women who share that same commitment. As a result, I have a larger portion of my time devoted to prayer than will be possible for many people.

You may, for example, be a mother with small children around the house. Or you may be a man or woman whose job occupies sixty or seventy hours of your week. Your life may go through different seasons: times when you have greater opportunity for prayer, other times when you have less, and some when it seems you have hardly any at all.

But though there are many differences in our lives, yet I believe that the elements of prayer I am going to share will be applicable, in one form or another, to all of us. As you read them, ask the Lord to show you the best way to incorporate them into your own particular set of circumstances.

The First Element: Praise

The first and most basic element of our prayer must be praise. It does not matter who we are, what our circumstances are, or what season of life we are in, the most fundamental thing we are to do is to praise and worship the Lord, our God, our King, our Creator.

The psalmist says, "I will bless the LORD at all times; his praise shall continually be in my mouth" (Ps 34:1). When he says "at all times," I believe he means *at all times*: good times, bad times, happy times, sorrowful times, busy times, leisurely times. The praise of God should always be in our hearts and on our lips.

That is a tall order. How are we to go about it? More specifically, where are we to find the words with which to praise God in this way?

I find that many people struggle with this problem. Much of my speaking ministry takes place in large meetings of people who are active in the charismatic renewal, and who are quite at home with vocal, exuberant praise and worship. But even among them I often notice a rather limited "praise vocabulary." Many of them, when they praise the Lord, simply say over and over again, "I praise you, Lord. I worship you. I praise you, Lord." If it were not for these few phrases, they might find themselves with a heart full of praise but no words with which to express it!

If our praise of the Lord is going to be as rich and full and joyful as it could be, we need to base it on the word of God. The Bible, particularly the Psalms, is an endless storehouse of inspired prayer with which to worship God.

The Psalms: The Basic Book of Prayer

I draw most of my praise from the psalms. Indeed, the Book of Psalms is the basic prayer collection of God's people—a collection directly inspired by the Holy Spirit. We can surmise that it is even the book from which Jesus drew most of his personal prayer.

Using the psalms, I might decide to focus my praise on the attributes of God. I might, for example, begin with Psalm 18:

> I love thee, O LORD, my strength.
> The LORD is my rock, and my fortress, and my deliverer,
>   my God, my rock, in whom I take refuge,
>   my shield, and the horn of my salvation, my stronghold.
> I call upon the LORD, who is worthy to be praised,
>   and I am saved from my enemies.
>   (Ps 18:1-3)

Then, in my prayer, I can personalize the words of the psalm:

> *I love you, Lord. You are my strength, my fortress, my deliverer. I take refuge in you, for you are a solid rock of refuge. You are the source of my salvation. You are worthy to be praised, and you save me from everything that would try to harm me.*

Similarly, I might use the psalms to focus on the great things God has done—and will continue to do—for me:

> Bless the LORD, O my soul;
>   and all that is within me, bless his holy name!
> Bless the LORD, O my soul,
>   and forget not all his benefits,
> who forgives all your iniquity,
>   who heals all your diseases,
> who redeems your life from the Pit,
>   who crowns you with steadfast love and mercy,
> who satisfies you with good as long as you live
>   so that your youth is renewed like the eagle's.
>   (Ps 103:1-5)

Again, it is a simple matter to adjust the words and make them my own: *I bless you Lord, because you forgive all my sins . . .*

A Personal Vocabulary of Praise

There are many other psalms—and many other passages of Scripture—that can provide a basis for our praise. I find it helpful to memorize such passages and to make it a point to use them for a while after memorizing them, so that they stay with me. Then, over a period of time, I build up a personal vocabulary of praise that I can draw on at any time, in any situation.

Another important ingredient of praise is music. Earlier I said that the Book of Psalms is a collection of prayers. That is true, but there is more to it than that. Actually, the Book of Psalms is a collection of hymns, of praise songs. Originally they were all set to music; and even now some of the best praise songs are actually psalms set to music.

If you can sing, then sing to the Lord when you praise him. If you can play an instrument, so much the better. If you are not musically inclined, don't worry. God doesn't expect us all to be virtuosos. He calls us to "make a joyful *noise*" to him (see Ps 66:1, Ps 100:1), and he takes delight in our efforts to glorify him, however raucous or refined they may be.

The Second Element: Absorbing God's Word

A second element of prayer that I want to highlight is reading Scripture. As we read God's word we learn more about who God is, how he acts, what his priorities are. One of the most basic ways we can grow in our life with God is by simply immersing ourselves in God's word.

I recommend that we set a goal for ourselves that we can actually attain—say, one or two chapters a day—and set about regularly reading the entire Bible in some systematic way. There are different ways to do this. The simplest is just to begin at Genesis 1:1 and read straight through the Bible, one or two chapters at a time, until we have completed Revelation 22:21. There are also a variety of simple Bible-reading plans available that can guide us through the entirety of Scripture over the course of a year.

Whatever system or method we adopt is not as important as the fact that we regularly expose ourselves to *everything* God has to say to us in his word. I emphasize *everything* because most of us, if we do not adopt a systematic approach, will tend to gravitate toward those sections of Scripture that we already know well. As a result we miss out on the sweep of God's revelation of himself and his plan.

I am regularly surprised, as I read through the Bible, at how many life-changing truths I come across that I would have missed entirely had I merely focused on my favorite familiar passages. There are some passages that now mean a great deal to me that I never would have found had I not committed myself to this approach.

Treasures Almost Overlooked

For example, Second Kings was not a book with which I had a great deal of familiarity in the past. It was not the first place it would occur to me to turn to when I wanted to sit down and read Scripture during my prayer time. But tucked away in chapter six is a passage that has come to be very meaningful to me.

The passage concerns the prophet Elisha. The Israelites are at war with the Assyrians, and at this particular point they seem to be hopelessly surrounded. Elisha's servant gets up one morning and looks around the Israelites' encampment, and "behold, an army with horses and chariots was round about the city." Talk about a rotten way to start the day! Elisha's servant cries out, "Alas, my master! What shall we do?"

Elisha answers him, "Fear not, for those who are with us are more than those who are with them." In others words, Elisha is saying, "Don't worry, our army is much larger than theirs."

This does not seem to comfort Elisha's servant, since all he can see with his natural eyes is the enemy army surrounding them. Elisha recognizes what the problem is: "Oh, I understand! He can't see what's really going on here!" He prays, "O Lord, open his eyes that he may see." And Scripture records that "the LORD opened the eyes of the young man, and he saw; and behold, the mountain was full of horses and chariots of fire round about Elisha" (see 2 Kgs 6:15-17).

What a marvelous account of God's presence with his people! It reminds me that even when I am in the midst of difficulty or danger, I am never alone. Even when everything I can see with my natural eyes seems to be against me, I am nevertheless surrounded by God's love.

I have called this passage to mind many, many times. It has been a great source of comfort and courage for me. And yet I might very well never have come across it had I not adopted the practice of systematically reading through the entire Bible.

Paul told Timothy—and he tells us as well—that "*all* Scripture is inspired by God and profitable for teaching, for reproof, for correction, and for training in righteousness, that the man [or woman] of God may be complete, equipped for every good work" (2 Tm 3:16). Let us then make full use of this great treasure God has given us, reading the entirety of God's word, reviewing the full panorama of his revelation, letting it all come to take root in our lives.

The Third Element: Meditation

A third element of personal prayer is meditating on Scripture.

Luke records that after Mary had given birth to Jesus, and had heard the heavenly host proclaiming him savior of the world, she "kept all these things, pondering them in her heart" (Lk 2:19). That is what we do when we meditate on God's word: we ponder it in our heart.

In addition to my daily "reading-through" of Scripture, I take time during prayer twice a week to meditate on a passage of Scripture. Often in the course of my reading the Lord will bring a particular passage to my attention, and make it "come alive" for me in a special way.

For example, a few years ago I sensed him bringing to my attention a verse from the letter to the Ephesians: "Therefore, putting away falsehood, let every one speak the truth with his neighbor, for we are members one of another" (Eph 4:25). I spent a few minutes just reading and rereading the passage, letting it sink in—learning it, as we sometimes say, "by heart."

I called the passage to mind several times during the next few days, trying to consider how it might apply to me in the actual circumstances of daily life. Then I went back to it during a later prayer time, reviewing what I had learned and making some resolutions to change my behavior where it seemed appropriate.

Let me give you an example of how this passage might be meditated upon:

The passage says to put away all falsehood. Is all falsehood gone from my life? Do I tell lies? What about "white lies?" Are there times when I bend the truth for the sake of social convenience? What about exaggeration? Do I allow myself to overstate things or to stretch the truth in order to make a point? God wants me to put away all falsehood. He wants me to speak the truth, so that when people talk to me they know they are hearing nothing that is not true.

The passage says we are to speak the truth to our neighbor. Am I completely open and straightforward in my dealings with others? Or do I hold back on speaking the truth, say, when I know I need to confront someone, because I don't want to risk getting a negative reaction?

The passage points out that my brothers and sisters and I are members one of another. We belong to one another. We have the same Father, the same Lord, the same Spirit. We are one body;

what affects one affects the others. That is why the truth is so
crucial. Do I keep this in mind in my dealings with brothers and
sisters?

And so it goes. This is an illustration of meditating upon
what I would call a teaching passage: one that sets forth a basic
principle of living. We can also meditate on other kinds of
passages. For example, we might meditate on a story from the
Gospels: reading it through, reflecting on its meaning, then
imagining ourselves actually being present in the events of the
story, hearing what is said, seeing what is done, considering
how we ourselves might have responded to different aspects of
it.

Whatever approach we take, meditation is a very good way to
help God's word get down deep inside us and take root, so that
it can bear more fruit in our lives.

The Fourth Element: Study

A fourth element of prayer is Scripture study.

I am not talking here about *academic* study, the kind of thing
we would do if were trying to earn a degree in theology. I am
talking about a more simple type of personal study, designed to
make the meaning of Scripture come alive for us in our prayer.

For most of us I would recommend pursuing this kind of
Scripture study on an occasional basis: not every day or every
week, perhaps, but at less frequent but regular intervals when
we sense the Lord wants to teach us more about a particular
portion of Scripture.

Let us say, for example, that I want to study a particular
chapter. I begin by reading it through several times, usually in
more than one translation, until I am familiar with the main
themes. I then write either an outline or a brief summary of
what the chapter says, restating its content in my own words
and noting how the various thoughts relate to another. Using
the cross-references supplied in my Bible, I note other passages

that shed light on the same points. I might also look up some of the key words in a Bible dictionary. Finally, I highlight one or more passages that seem to express particularly well the main points being made; I often use these passages for meditation during the coming weeks.

This entire process need take no more than an hour. But it is well worth the effort because of the greatly increased understanding of God's word that it yields.

Incidentally, I have described this as a simple method of *personal* Scripture study, but many people find it helpful to study Scripture together with other brothers and sisters. This can be done using the same method I have described, by having each member of the group share the insights he or she has gleaned from personal study. Or the group might want to use one of the many good Bible study booklets that are available or even listen to tapes and discuss them together.

The Backbone of a Life of Prayer

These, then, are some important elements of personal prayer. But only *some*. Prayer is an inexhaustible topic. An entire book could be written—indeed, many entire books *have* been written—about the ways of prayer. You may already have some of the elements I have described incorporated into your prayer life. You may be doing them in a somewhat different manner than I have described. You may find that you make use of other disciplines and patterns when you pray.

In the end, it does not matter so much what particular system or approach we adopt. What does matter is that we pray: that we keep our spiritual life in good running condition by regularly spending time in God's presence, pouring ourselves out to him in love, receiving his wisdom, love, correction, and encouragement in return. What does matter is that we fulfill our "joyful duty." The precise manner in which we fulfill it can vary.

Nevertheless, I think it is fair to say that almost any approach to personal prayer will in some way reflect the elements I have outlined: praise and worship of God, meditation, reading, and study of his word in Scripture. These elements help form the backbone of a life of prayer, which is in turn the backbone of a life of love. Yet there is one more element that needs to be mentioned, one more component of a life of prayer that is so important I need to devote considerably more space to it. Let us turn now to this most important additional element of prayer.

SIX

Standing in the Gap

M OST OF US, IF WE ARE HONEST, will confess that our personal prayer times are rather ... well, they are rather *ordinary* most of the time.

We get up at the usual time, go to the usual place, sit in the usual chair and drink the usual cup of coffee. After years, perhaps, of daily prayer, we have settled into a pattern of prayer that helps us make contact with the Lord. Most of the time nothing terribly spectacular goes on. Ordinary. Routine.

But have you ever considered what an awesome privilege prayer is?

Have you ever considered what an incredible thing it is that you and I—*you* and *I*, of all people—can come into the very presence of the God of the universe? Can speak to him? Can pour out our joys and sorrows to him? Can read his word in the Bible? Can sit at his feet and listen to him speak directly to our hearts by the working of the Holy Spirit?

Yet all of that is precisely what happens each and every time we pray—no matter how "ordinary" the outward circumstances of our prayer time may seem. We come into the presence of the living God. We encounter him person-to-person. We converse with him. We draw life and power and wisdom from him.

What Is Intercession?

In the last chapter I discussed several basic elements of a personal prayer time. You may have noticed that I failed to mention one of the most important elements of all. It is the one that enables us not just to grow in God's love for ourselves, but to extend his love and mercy and power to others. It is intercession. Like the other elements I mentioned, intercession should be part of our prayer on a regular basis.

What is intercession? The dictionary defines the verb *to intercede* as "to act between parties with a view to reconciling differences; to beg or plead on behalf of another; to mediate."

Jesus is *the* Intercessor. He is the Mediator between God and man. His death and resurrection served as the definitive act that reconciled the differences between God and man. And now, reigning as he does at the Father's right hand in the eternal kingdom, Jesus continues to mediate on our behalf. He pleads our case at the Father's throne and answers our prayers, sending us his Holy Spirit, his grace, his favor.

As Christians, we unite with the intercession of Jesus by praying for particular people and particular needs. When we beg God for mercy, or plead with the Lord on behalf of another, we are joining Jesus' intercession. We are uniting our prayer for that person or that need with Jesus' eternal, unending intercession. God answers our prayer because Jesus, our Mediator, is pleading our case before the Father.

Scripture tells us that Jesus "always lives to make intercession" for us (Heb 7:25). When our prayers are united with the intercession of our Lord Jesus Christ, they come before the throne of God, and our Father answers them.

What Is an Intercessor?

It is easy to get the wrong idea about what an intercessor is. We might think that an intercessor is one who grits his teeth and digs in to pray for hours. But that is not necessarily true. An intercessor is not just someone who prays longer or more intensely. Rather, a true intercessor is one who makes *a long-term decision to plead on behalf of another.*

In Ezekiel 22:30, God asks through the prophet for people to "stand in the gap" for others. That vivid phrase helps to capture the essence of intercession. God's plea that more people become intercessors shows what a crucial and neglected role it is. Indeed, there are a number of passages in Scripture that tell us how much the Lord looks to his people to "stand in the gap" for others.

One such passage is in the book of Isaiah. "The Lord saw [the wickedness of the people], and it displeased him that there was no justice. He saw that there was no man, and *wondered that there was no one to intervene*" (Is 59:15-16).

What a tragedy! God could find no one to intervene, to intercede, to plead before him for mercy on behalf of the people. Is the same thing true today? Or are there men and women of God prepared to stand in the gap?

In the book of Ezekiel the Lord says, "And I sought for a man among them who should build up the wall and stand in the breach before me for the land, that I should not destroy it; *but I found none*. Therefore I have poured out my indignation upon them; I have consumed them with the fire of my wrath; their way have I requited upon their heads, says the Lord GOD" (Ez 22:30-31).

Imagine: just one person, pleading with God, could have saved that nation from judgment. That is the power of intercession. That is the value God places on it.

It is true that only the Savior, the Messiah, the Lord Jesus perfectly fulfills those two Scripture passages I have just quoted. But it is equally true that God wants us to join in prayer with Jesus standing in the gap for those without faith, those in sin, those too ill to pray.

A Powerful Tool

Today the Lord is asking you and me to intercede. We all know the condition of our world: the painful problems of violence, poverty, lust, greed, and all the rest. Everyone is affected by such problems. Moreover, we know the particular problems faced by members of our families. And who among us does not have problems in our own life?

God looks at our problems and tells us that he has given us a powerful tool, one that can move mountains: the power of intercessory prayer.

It is hard for us to believe this. We are the "instant generation." We push a button and a bank machine places cash in our hands. We open a box and our dinner appears.

I am not opposed to the conveniences of modern life. But when the "instant results" mentality infects our view of prayer, we can get into difficulty. We often do not see instant results. God frequently works in a different way because he demands change from human beings, both in the one praying and in the one being prayed for. If we have expected instant results, we can easily become discouraged and give up too soon. Intercession requires perseverance.

We also have to resist the temptation of saying, "I'm too busy to pray that much," or, "God may be calling someone else to that, but not me." The fact of the matter is that God calls *each and every one of us* to intercede. The New Testament is full of exhortations to pray (see, for example, 1 Thes 5:17 and 1 Tm 2:1-4). Christian teaching through the ages likewise contains exhortation after exhortation to pray.

God does not present intercession as an option. It is a duty that comes right along with the many privileges of being his children.

Once I was speaking on intercession at a conference, and I asked the rhetorical question, "Who will stand in the gap?" A four-year-old boy jumped up and said, "I will!" *Out of the mouths of babes*... I thought as I stood looking at his eager little face. We are all called to respond with that same enthusiasm.

Will God look upon our generation and be forced to say, "I looked for one to intervene, but I found no one?" Or, "I searched for someone to stand in the breach, but found none?"

Or will he see a people before him, pleading for his mercy for this generation, this nation, this world?

Who among us will answer his call?

Requirements for Intercessors: Personal Repentance

When we come before the Lord to intercede, we must first of all repent of our sins. We cannot expect to engage in fruitful intercession, asking God to do all manner of things for ourselves, for our families, for others, unless we are in right standing before the Lord.

"The prayer of a righteous man has great power in its effects," writes James (Jas 5:16). We become righteous when we repent of our sins and beg God in his mercy to bestow his righteousness upon us. This is how we get into the right place before God. "If we confess our sins, he is faithful and just, and will forgive our sins and cleanse us from all unrighteousness" (1 Jn 1:9). The frame of mind and heart that enables us to intercede effectively comes from a repentant heart.

Over the years, God has touched my own heart time and again, always going deeper, always showing me more that I can repent for. Does that sound grim and uninviting? Actually, it is just the opposite. There is tremendous joy in repentance. I believe I am at the point today where I can honestly say, "Please *do* show me my sin, Lord." Every time I repent, I know more of God. Every time I repent, I have more of God's life in me: more of his joy, more of his peace, more of his presence, more of his hope. These blessings are the fruit of repentance.

When we come before the Lord to pray for others, for the serious needs we have, we must first repent of our own sins. We must be humble; we must be sorry; we must be willing to change. Those who are Catholic should regularly avail themselves of the Sacrament of Reconciliation. Thus do we become "righteous men and women" whose prayer will have "great power in its effects."

The Scriptures challenge us to boldness in intercession. We

are to stand in the gap and confront the living God, pleading for his mercy and grace. The only way to do this, considering how awesome our God is, is by being humble and repentant.

Requirements for Intercessors: Praying as Part of God's People

We must also learn to intercede *as a part of God's people*. We do not come before the Lord simply as isolated individuals. We do it as part of the larger community to which we belong: the body of Christ.

Because we are all members together of the one body, we share in the condition of God's people, apart from our own personal condition. Individually we may not be guilty of greed or lust or violence. But because some of our brothers and sisters are, we share in the consequences they bring upon all of us. It is important that we understand our relationship to others in this way and intercede from that relationship.

An example of this is provided by Moses. Shortly after God had miraculously delivered the chosen people from their slavery in Egypt, they committed some terrible sins. Moses was not involved in the wrongdoing. Nevertheless, he accepted his share in the people's predicament and interceded accordingly:

> Moses said to the people, "You have sinned a great sin. And now I will go up to the LORD; perhaps I can make atonement for your sin." So Moses returned to the LORD and said, "Alas, this people have sinned a great sin; they have made for themselves gods of gold. But now, if thou wilt forgive their sin—and if not, blot me, I pray thee, out of thy book which thou hast written." (Ex 32:30-32)

Moses begged the Lord to grant forgiveness to the people. But if the Lord was not willing to forgive, Moses wanted to receive the same punishment the people were to receive, even though he had not committed the sin. He knew he was a part of that people, and that he shared their lot in life. He was willing to stand in the gap completely, even suffering punishment if that was to be God's response.

In the same way, we are part of God's people, and we have a share in the condition of God's people. Even if we do not approve of what is going on, even if we ourselves are free of blame, we share in the responsibility for what occurs—both the good and the bad. We are called to stand with our brothers and sisters as we stand in the gap. We do this by asking for God's mercy and God's blessings on all of God's people, on the whole church around the world.

We are called to understand our share in the condition of mankind. We are also called to do what Moses did: he did not turn his back on his people; rather, he went up to the Lord as a representative of his people, interceding on their behalf.

Requirements for Intercessors: Repenting on Behalf of Others

Once these attitudes of personal repentance and identification with God's people are part of our lives, we are able to *repent on behalf of God's people*. Nehemiah provides a striking example of this aspect of intercession:

"O LORD God of heaven, the great and terrible God who keeps covenant and steadfast love with those who love him and keep his commandments; let thy ear be attentive, and thy eyes open, to hear the prayer of thy servant which I now pray before thee day and night for the people of Israel thy servants, confessing the sins of the people of Israel, which we have sinned against thee. Yea, I and my father's house have sinned. We have acted very corruptly against thee, and have not kept the commandments, the statutes, and the ordinances which thou didst command thy servant Moses."

(Neh 1:5-7)

Nehemiah was not saying that he himself had committed all those sins. He was praying in repentance for all of God's people, begging the Lord's forgiveness and mercy on everyone—on himself, his relatives, and the entire people of God.

When we come before the Lord, we too can and should ask God's mercy and forgiveness on all his people. God honors such prayer. He hears and responds to it.

In the book of Ezra we find a similar prayer:

"O my God, I am ashamed and blush to lift my face to thee, my God, for our iniquities have risen higher than our heads, and our guilt has mounted up to the heavens. From the days of our fathers to this day we have been in great guilt." (Ezr 9:6-7)

The priest Ezra goes on to beg God to have mercy on the Israelites, to forgive them their sins. Ezra himself was a righteous man. He had not committed all these sins. Yet he repented, both personally and on behalf of all God's people.

May the Lord teach us from these Scriptures to offer prayers of repentance on behalf of all those deep in sin! God will hear our prayers of humble repentance. He will answer them.

Praying according to God's Mind and Heart

As we begin to take on the appropriate attitude, recognizing that we are part of God's people and are one with them in their joy and sorrow, in their righteousness and in their sin; as we resolve that we are going to pray for them no matter what they have done; as we build our prayer on a base of personal repentance; then we put ourselves in the place where we can begin to pray according to God's mind and heart, and God will hear and answer our prayer.

We have many scriptural models to guide us. Remember Abraham's prayer for Sodom and Gomorrah. Remember Moses' prayer that the people be spared from the plagues. Remember Ezra and Nehemiah and David. Remember how

Jesus prayed for his disciples, and how they prayed for those they brought into the Christian family.

All these were righteous men who stood in the gap, who interceded for others before the throne of God. And God heard their prayers.

We are called to pray in a similar way. Not in self-righteousness, but with humble and contrite hearts. When we do, the Lord will hear and answer our prayers.

The Lord told Isaiah the prophet: "This is the man to whom I will look, he that is humble and contrite in spirit, and trembles at my word" (Is 66:2). We need to take these words to heart, and let them guide our intercession.

Intercession Is Important to God

Some years ago, when I first began to speak at large Christian conferences, I was impressed at how challenging it could be to get up before thousands of people and speak. I realized that if I was going to tell people what God expected of them, I would have to practice what I preached! I knew I would need God's help if I were to succeed.

About three years after I started speaking, I had a particularly important encounter. A woman came up to me after one of my talks and said, "You don't know me; we've never met. But I feel I know you. One evening about three years ago I was praying, and I sensed the Lord telling me to commit myself to pray for you. I want you to know that I *have* been praying for you, regularly, for three years. I've been asking the Lord to give you the grace to remain faithful to him, to do what he wants you to do."

How important intercession is to the Lord! It is so important that he provides intercessors for us—sometimes even people we do not know. I know I never would have been able to do the things I have done, to be of service to God's people in the ministries he has called me to, were it not for people like that woman interceding for me.

If God places this much value on intercession, so should we.

Every committed Christian has been called by the Lord to pray for someone or something. Maybe it is your spouse and children, your parents, your friends, your pastor or another Christian leader. Most likely God calls you to pray for those involved in wrongdoing and for the victims of their sin. Whoever or whatever he calls you to intercede for, do it!

What Does God Want You to Pray For?

Let me encourage you to assess your own situation and determine what the Lord wants *you* to intercede for.

Here is a simple way to begin. Think for a moment about needs you are aware of in your family, in the church (perhaps in your parish), and in the world. Choose one particular need in each of these three areas. Then go to the Lord and say, "Lord, how do you want me to pray?"

Then decide on a day (or days) of the week that you can designate for intercession. Determine what time of day, and what place of prayer, will work best for you. I know people who intercede while they are driving to work. I know others who set aside a particular time during the day at work or at home. It doesn't really matter where or when you do it, so long as you can be relatively free from distractions.

We can also ask the Lord how we might fast as part of our intercession. I think fasting says to God, "I'm willing to put aside the time I would spend satisfying my bodily comforts and use that time to take on God's concerns—praying for his people." Again, the particulars of fasting can vary: whether we fast from dessert, or from lunch, or from all three meals on a given day, and so on. Different approaches will be appropriate for different people, depending on age, health, and circumstances. But I urge you to incorporate fasting into your intercession as God directs. It also underlines the prayer of your heart.

This simple exercise—choosing a handful of specific needs, praying for them at the same time and in the same place each week, fasting as appropriate—will help you grow as an intercessor. You will find, as you are faithful to the program God gives you, that he will also give you more faith, more hope, more love for those for whom you are praying.

Intercession is like any other discipline. The more you do it, the better you get at it. And, as we have seen from Scripture, God wants us to become very good intercessors.

Intercessors: Spiritual Warriors

God wants spiritual warriors: men and women who are serious, committed, fervent intercessors. God is extending an invitation to us—an invitation which, if we accept it, can free us from anxiety, frustration, and pain. He is offering us a tool to take into our hands and use to build his kingdom. We no longer need to throw up our hands in despair about situations that trouble us. We no longer need to ask, "What can I do?" when confronted with a need in our family. Intercession is a powerful weapon. We can use it and see great results.

Several years ago the Lord spoke a prophetic word, a portion of which I would like to share with you here because I think it is as true today as when it was first given:

> *I want to see before me on their knees a people humble and repentant. Teach my people to pray. Teach them to call upon my name earnestly, ceaselessly, and with faith. Teach them to wage war through their prayer upon an enemy who wanders up and down through their ranks, destroying and devouring. Teach them to ask mercy for themselves, their brothers, and their sisters. . . . Pray with fasting, pray with vigils, pray with earnestness. For the sake of a even a few, I will be merciful to many.*

Who will stand in the gap? Who will intervene for *your* family, for *your* church, for the state of the world? I believe God is issuing an invitation as well as a command. Who will answer? How can we pass up the opportunity, the challenge, the ministry God holds out to us? I beg you to take God's word seriously.

SEVEN

Praying for Those We Love

PERHAPS YOU ARE ONE OF THE MANY PEOPLE who have been praying for someone close to you for years without seeming to have received an answer to your prayers. I have met many such people. They are praying for their children, or for someone who is sick, or for the mending of a broken family relationship. They get discouraged because they do not see results.

If you are one these people, let me urge you not to give in to discouragement. Let me assure you of one crucial truth: *God hears every word you pray, and he answers every one of your prayers.* His answers may not always come in the form you expect, or as soon as you would like. But the prayers of faithful sons and daughters of God are *always* answered—without fail.

The Fruit of Faithful Intercession

A few years ago I was talking with a young woman who had given her life to the Lord four years before, while she was in college. As she described herself, she did not sound like a promising candidate for conversion. She was living a very ungodly lifestyle. She had flatly rejected her parents' Christianity. She had left home on two previous occasions and was on the verge of deciding to do so again.

"In reality," she told me, "my life was miserable. But I liked doing what I wanted, when I wanted, and I didn't want to give that up."

Then one day someone spoke to her about God's love for her, about his readiness to forgive her. Somehow the message that she had resisted so many times before mananged to penetrate her heart—just a little. She went home in some turmoil. As she lay on her bed, listening to rock music, trying to drown out the disturbing message, she suddenly got the strange feeling that someone was in the room with her, watching her.

She sat up, looked around the room; there was no one.

She got up and explored the house. Still she found no one. But she could not shake the feeling that someone was watching her.

"I tried to reason it out," she told me. "If someone was looking at me, but there was no one in the house, then the someone had to be God. So I asked God if it was him."

She heard the answer clearly: "Yes." Within moments she responded to God's grace and gave her life to the Lord right then and there. Without even turning off the rock music, she began praying. The Lord baptized her in the Holy Spirit and she prayed in tongues for a half hour, not even understanding what she was doing.

A while later her mother came home. The girl knew her mother had been praying for her for several years. She asked her mother to come to her room.

"Mom," she said, "I have something important to tell you."

"What is it?" her mother asked—expecting to hear that her daughter was planning to leave home yet again.

"I just gave my life to God," the girl said. "I love God. And I love you."

This mother and one of her friends had been fasting and praying together every Wednesday for years. They had been interceding for their children, praying that they would come to know Jesus Christ as their Lord. Now the mother was seeing the fruit of her faithful intercession.

God Always Answers Our Prayers

Often we come before God in prayer with our minds and spirits burdened by the needs of those we love. This one needs a job. This one is struggling with a difficult marriage. This one is ill. The needs are so great, the pain so real, that we cannot see beyond them. Our prayer consists mainly of rattling off a long list of petitions: Lord, change this. Lord, change that. Lord, do this. Lord, *help*.

Many people report, in some frustration, that God does not seem to answer their prayers. Now, on the one hand we must note that this is a very difficult thing to say accurately. We may not be getting the result we want, in the form we want, on the schedule we want. But that does not mean that God has not heard and answered our prayer. His answer may be, "Yes, but not now." Or it may be, "Yes, but not in that form."

Or it may simply be, "No." Do you realize that even "no" is a gracious answer from a merciful God? He knows our needs, and the needs of our loved ones, better than we do; and he sees better than we how all the problems and circumstances of life interact as part of his master plan. There are times when he knows that "no" is a better answer to our requests than "yes."

Getting to the Heart of the Matter

Nevertheless, it does seem that most of us are less effective, less fruitful, in intercessory prayer than we might be. One major reason, I think, has to do with our lack of perspective in prayer. We pray according to our limited mind, our limited vision, our limited understanding of what is best for the person. But what we really need is to pray according to God's mind, God's vision, God's understanding of what is best.

God wants us to be able to ask, not "What do I want to see happen for this person?" but "What does the Lord want to see happen for this person?" When you and I look at a situation, we focus on the obvious, immediate need. We want to see a job turn up for this one. We want to see this marriage reconciled.

We want to see this wayward son or daughter return. We want to see health for this one who is sick.

God wants those things, too, of course. But often he wants so much *more* besides, and he wants to go about it in such a different—and more glorious—way. God sees to the heart of the matter. He asks, Where does this person stand in relationship to me? Where do they stand in the family of God? Is this person one of my children? Is he or she ready to stand before me and be welcomed into my kingdom forever? God certainly wants to meet our here-and-now human needs. But he wants first and foremost to bring each of us into right relationship with him so we will be able to live with him for all eternity and share the fullness of life he has for us.

Three Questions that Point the Way

Thus if we are to intercede with power and fruitfulness, we must have God's mind and pray according to God's priorities for our loved ones. That is the first step. When we do this, we will become more and more able to see as God sees, to think and understand as God does, and thus to pray according to God's heart. The result will be greater spiritual blessing—and ultimately greater material blessing—for those we love. To adapt a principle from a familiar Scripture passage, when we seek first his kingdom and his righteousness for those we love, all these other things will be added unto them as well (see Mt 6:33).

In trying to learn to see things from God's perspective, I have found it helpful to ask myself three questions about the people for whom I am praying:

—Have they repented of sin? Are they living a life of humility before God?

—Do they know Jesus Christ as their personal Lord and Savior? Do they allow him to reign over every aspect of their lives? Do they live lives of obedience and gratitude?

—Have they surrendered their lives to the action of the Holy Spirit? Are they in a position to receive the gifts and graces of the Spirit that enable us to live the Christian life in peace and joy?

If the answer to any of these questions is anything other than a clear yes, then that immediately helps us point our intercessory prayer in the right direction. Repentance, faith, and the power of the Spirit are foundational to living the kind of life that can be fully blessed by God.

God wants to meet our financial, emotional, social, and other human needs, to be sure; but he first of all wants us in right relationship with him. Those are his priorities; they should be ours as well. Thus, even though it is perfectly appropriate for us to pray for any and all needs our loved ones may have, we should pray first and foremost for their spiritual welfare.

Short-term Pain, Long-term Gain

I believe we must even be willing to say to God, "Lord, I want my loved ones to belong to you. I want them to know the life and truth and goodness you have for them. My loved ones are in great difficulty now, and I long to see them set free. But Lord, if you need to use this difficult situation to bring them to yourself—or even just to bring them closer to yourself—then I unite my heart with yours. Whatever needs to happen to those I love, Lord, in order that they might repent, and come to know you as Savior, and surrender to your Lordship and to the power of your Spirit—Lord, let it be."

To pray this way requires faith in God's goodness and in his loving plan for each of our lives. God *wants* to bless us, to heal us, to care for us. But he wants our *ultimate* good, life with him forever, not just our short-term comfort. He is willing to reprove, chastise, and discipline us to bring us through trials and difficulties, if that will advance his ultimate goals.

We need to be able to surrender our loved ones to God's plan. We need to love them enough to do that. Jesus knows what our loved ones can endure. He will not let them be tempted beyond their strength (see 1 Cor 10:13). He hates to see our loved ones suffer—no doubt even more than we do. After all, they are *his* loved ones, too! But because he has the Father's priorities, he can lead them through difficulty if that is what is best for them, rather than simply remove the difficulty and let them continue in blindness or sin or settling for less than God desires for them.

I admit that it took me a long time to reach a point where I could pray this way. As I looked around at my loved ones, I could come up with long lists of things to pray for regarding every one of them. And they were good things, legitimate things. But gradually God began to help me focus on his priorities, to see my loved ones and their circumstances from his perspective, so that I could pray for them according to his mind and heart, not just my own.

Healing the Blindness of Pride

Let me describe in greater detail what it might mean to pray according to the three sets of questions I shared before.

The first question had to do with repentance. One thing we might pray about in this regard is that pride be removed from the person we are concerned for: the pride that keeps them from acknowledging or confessing their sin.

I am all too aware of how this works. I had an area of sin in my own life that I could not recognize as sin for many years. I thought of it simply as a "problem." Then one day God asked me how I thought *he* viewed my "problem." I could see right away that he viewed it as sin, and that it was nothing but my own pride that had stopped me from acknowledging it before.

I confessed that my sin really was sin, and I told the Lord I wanted to be done with it. With his help, and with counsel from a wise friend, I was able gradually to eliminate that sin from my life. But the indispensable first step was overcoming the pride that had prevented me from seeing my "problem" for what it really was. In the same way we can pray for those we love, that God will deal with their pride and remove the blindness that stops them from acknowledging their need for repentance.

Sending Just the Right Person

Another thing we can pray for regarding repentance is that the Lord send just the right person into the life of the one we are praying for: someone who will be able to speak the truth to them in a way they can accept. You probably know as well as I do that our own family members can sometimes be the hardest people for us to confront with the truth. I often pray that other people will come into the life of the person I am praying for and speak the truth to them in a way that I cannot do, simply because of the closeness of family.

I recently heard an account of someone who allowed God to use her as "the right person" in the life of someone else. The story centers around a woman who had spent more than a decade in a psychiatric hospital following the trauma of living with an abusive husband. Her situation seemed hopeless. Her family members felt paralyzed: they wanted to help her, but they either could not think of how to do so or were unable to bring themselves to do so. They just prayed that somehow God would find a way to help her.

It was at this point that one of the woman's friends got involved. She sensed in prayer that the Lord wanted to use her as an instrument of his healing. She prayed, asking for guidance as to what she should do and how she should go about it. She consulted with the woman's psychiatrist and with her minister. When she felt confident that she had heard the Lord correctly, she went to the hospital, sat down with the troubled woman, took a deep breath, and gave her the message she felt God had sent her to give.

"I believe that God's desire is that you make a decision to forgive your husband," she said. "You are in bondage to hatred, bitterness, and revenge. Until you decide to forgive him for everything wrong he did to you, no matter how bad it was, you will not be free. But if you *do* make that decision, you *will* be free."

Can you see how hard it would have been for a member of the woman's family—who knew the details of her past so well, and who themselves were no doubt resentful against the abusive husband as well—to say these things? It was the second woman's detachment from the situation that enabled her to hear the Lord clearly and respond to him confidently. She was the right person for the Lord to send into this difficult situation. She was able to speak the truth.

And it worked! The troubled woman heard and embraced the message her friend brought her. She decided to forgive her husband from her heart, to set aside all bitterness and resentment against him. Within a matter of weeks she was released from the hospital where she had been for more than ten years. Certainly ongoing counseling and help were still needed, but the bondage to hatred was broken.

That story helps me remember, when I am praying for someone close to me who I know needs to repent and who cannot see their own need, that I can ask the Lord to send someone into their life who can speak the truth to them more effectively than I could.

Breaking the Bondage of Self

The second question I recommended that we ask regarding those we are praying for, as a foundation for asking God to meet their needs, is, Do they know Jesus Christ as their personal Lord and Savior?

Here, too, we often need to pray against pride in the form of self-sufficiency and self-reliance. Surely those of us who have already accepted Jesus as Lord know how this works! Life teaches us to be proud, to be self-sufficient and self-reliant. It teaches that we shouldn't need anyone but ourselves to run our lives—that if we do it is a sign of weakness.

Obviously there is nothing that will do a better job of standing between us and God than this attitude, and nothing that will more effectively prevent our loved ones from surrendering to Christ. This kind of pride tells us that we can save ourselves, when we cannot. It tells us we can know what is best for us, when we cannot. It tells us we can effectively control and direct our own lives, when we cannot. It tells us, in effect, that we can be our own gods—and that is one thing we certainly cannot be.

Acknowledging the Savior

I have found it effective, when praying that those I love would be able to surrender their lives to Christ's lordship, to pray against the lies of the evil one that work so powerfully to lead us astray: "I don't need anyone or anything. I can handle things all by myself." "I can get it together by myself; I just need a little more time." It is Satan who prompts us—and those we love—to think this way. But through the death and resurrection of Jesus, God enables us to break the power of these lies, both in our own lives and in the lives of those we are interceding for.

God knows how desperately we need a Savior, how desperately we need to surrender our lives to his Son's lordship. What else is it but pride that prevents us from acknowledging the one who alone can save and deliver us? The one who alone can be Lord of our lives?

How many of us have seen the joy on the faces of men and women who have opened themselves to God's grace and have said, "I can't do it on my own, Lord. I want to live a good life, but I can't do it alone. I need your help. Jesus, Son of the living

God, come and save me. Be Lord of my life. I give you full access to every part of me. Come into my life. Reign over me. Lead me to the Father."

When people have prayed this way from their hearts, their whole lives have changed: their minds, their emotions, their hearts, their souls, even their physical bodies. Light and strength flow into them, a new hope transforms them. This is what we are praying will happen for those we love. And God wants to do it; it is the deepest desire of his heart for those we love. For this reason we can pray for it with confidence.

Releasing the Power of the Spirit

The third question is, Have they opened their lives to the full working of the Holy Spirit?

Here I think our prayers are often too narrow. We tend to think that other people can come into an experience of the Holy Spirit only by following the same route that we followed. If we encountered a new release of the Spirit at a particular kind of prayer meeting, then we assume they will have to go to the same kind of prayer meeting. If we experienced the release of the Spirit at a seven-week seminar, then we assume that they will have to attend a seven-week seminar.

Now I am certainly not saying we should *avoid* introducing our friends and loved ones to the same experiences that we found helpful. But we need to be careful not to limit our conception of where and how the Holy Spirit can work. We can wear ourselves out trying to manufacture what we think are "just the right circumstances" rather than simply pray in faith to the Lord. God is so much bigger and more powerful than our puny ideas of him—and so much more flexible and inventive than we sometimes give him credit for!

One of our greatest pitfalls, especially when praying for family and friends, is to think that we know just exactly how everything needs to happen. And so we pray that things will happen in a very particular way. Now, that may be exactly the way that God does indeed wish to work. But it may not be. It may, in fact, be the case that the thing we are praying for is the very thing that would prevent our friends from experiencing what God has for them.

We need simply to pray, consistently and persistently, for the release of the Holy Spirit in our loved ones' lives. We need to let God answer that prayer however and whenever and wherever and through whomever he chooses, knowing that God knows and loves our friends and family members even better than we do. He wants them to come to repentance, faith, and life in the Spirit even more than we want it. And he knows far better than we do how to bring it to pass.

Seek First His Kingdom

It can be very difficult to adopt this approach to intercessory prayer. When we look at the situations of those dear to us, we see their needs and the problems so clearly; they press in on us so strongly. Surely that is where the bulk of the intercession should be focused!

I am not saying that we should not pray for such things. I am simply saying that the key to intercession is keeping first things first. I am simply applying to intercessory prayer the same lesson that Jesus taught us about seeking our own needs:

"Therefore I tell you, do not be anxious about your life, what you shall eat or what you shall drink, nor about your body, what you shall put on. Is not life more than food, and the body more than clothing?

"Look at the birds of the air: they neither sow nor reap nor gather into barns, and yet your heavenly Father feeds them. Are you not of more value than they? And which of you by being anxious can add one cubit to his span of life? And why are you anxious about clothing? Consider the lilies of the field, how they grow; they neither toil nor spin; yet I tell you, even Solomon in all his glory was not arrayed like one of these. But if God so clothes the grass of the field, which today is alive and tomorrow is thrown into the oven, will he

not much more clothe you, O men of little faith?
Therefore do not be anxious, saying, 'What shall we eat?' or
'What shall we drink?' or 'What shall we wear?' For the
Gentiles seek all these things; and your heavenly Father
knows that you need them all. *But seek first his kingdom and
his righteousness, and all these things shall be yours as well."* (Mt
6:25-33)

Do you see how it works? The Lord already knows
everything that we need and everything that our families need,
our wives, our husbands, our children, and our friends. Our
job, in interceding for them, is to "seek first his kingdom and
his righteousness" for them. And then all the other things will
be theirs as well.

No Time Like the Present

Let me encourage you, as you embark on the great ministry
of intercessory prayer, to take these words of Jesus to heart and
to have confidence that God *always* hears us when we call to
him.

Perhaps reading this chapter has called to mind friends or
family members who are in need and has prompted you to pray
for them. Go ahead! "Behold, now is the acceptable time;
behold, now is the day of salvation" (2 Cor 6:2). In fact, let me
offer you a few words of petition and intercession to help you
get started:

*Lord, you know the needs of those I love. You know the pain.
You know the fear. You know the anxiety and the struggle. I
know, Lord, that what they need most is to come to you. Bring
them to yourself, Lord, that they may have fullness of life in you.
Show me how to pray for them, so that they may receive everything
that you have for them, in the way and in the time that you have
ordained. O Lord, hear my prayer and let my cry come unto you.
Amen.*

EIGHT

An Essential Key to Effective Intercession

A LL OF US, WHEN WE PRAY, want our prayers to be effective. Of course: why else would we do it? And yet we often feel, rightly or wrongly, that we are not being as fruitful in our intercessory prayer as we could be. What is the key to effective intercession in our personal lives?

When I think about men and women whose prayer has power, I think about men and women who know and love and obey the will of God. I think about men and women who know God's word, and cherish it, and desire to follow it. *Obedience* is the key to effective intercession.

Jesus, during the last few hours before he was to be delivered up to death, made a remarkable statement to his disciples: "If you abide in me, and my words abide in you, ask whatever you will, and it shall be done for you" (Jn 15:7).

What a profound promise! "Ask *whatever* you will, and it shall be done for you." Another translation puts it even more plainly and dramatically: "If you remain in me and my words remain in you, you may ask what you will, and *you shall get it.*"

But there is a condition: "*If* you abide in me, and my words abide in you." To abide means to live in, to dwell in, to be at home in, to be comfortable in. Does God's word abide in your daily life? Is it at home there? Can God's word dwell comfortably in your daily thoughts, words, and actions? In other words, is your life characterized by obedience to God's word? Obedience is the key to intercession: it is when we obey that we may "ask what we will" with such extravagant confidence.

In this chapter I would like to share some thoughts about obedience: about what it can mean for us, how it can change us, and how it can help us live a life of love and prayer.

Obedience Saved My Life

I was about seven years old, as I recall. There had been a big thunderstorm this particular day, and as a result there was a small river of water flowing down the gutter and into the storm sewer. I was sitting outside along the curb, making little paper boats and floating them down the street.

Now mind you, all I was doing was sitting there playing. I was not doing anything wrong, was not bothering anybody. So it came as a surprise when my great aunt suddenly appeared on the front porch and began calling out to me. "Come here!" she commanded. "Come here! Quick! I want you up here on the porch with me right now!"

I can still remember sitting there, listening to her, and debating—just for a moment—whether or not I was going to do what she was asking me to do. I finally decided that I would, and so I hopped up from the curb and ran to the porch.

Just then a car came careening around the corner, swerving from side to side, tires squealing. We later learned that the driver was drunk. He was going much too fast to hold the curve, and his car smashed into a telephone pole at the very spot where I had been sitting a moment before.

You can probably imagine the look I gave my great aunt, and how glad I was that I had decided to obey her! Later she told me she had just sensed that there was danger near and she wanted me near her. I learned a big lesson that day about obedience: I learned that sometimes it can save your life.

Obedience Brings Eternal Life

Obedience can save not only our natural life, but also our eternal life. The Lord himself speaks about this in the Old Testament:

> "I call heaven and earth to witness against you this day, that I have set before you life and death, blessing and curse; therefore choose life, that you and your descendants may live, loving the LORD your God, obeying his voice, and cleaving to him; for that means life to you and length of days, that you may dwell in the land which the LORD swore to your fathers, to Abraham, to Isaac, and to Jacob, to give them." (Dt 30:19-20)

In this chapter of the book of Deuteronomy, the Lord speaks of the great blessings that come to those who obey him, who heed his voice and follow what he asks of them. The blessing for the Israelites is to inherit the promised land. For us, that translates into the blessing of inheriting eternal life.

Obedience Brings Fullness of Life

Obedience brings life. What is more, obedience brings *fullness* of life. It brings a depth and richness that comes from nothing else.

When I was a teenager I attended a public high school in our area. It was a good school, but I knew that deep down my parents really wanted me to have some Catholic education before I graduated.

It was during the summer before my junior year that I found out just how much they wanted it. They wanted it enough to send me to a boarding school for the next two years, since there was no Catholic school near us.

Well, I knew what that was going to mean. A strange place.

Strange people. Strange environment. New teachers. New friends.

No way.

I argued and fought. I didn't want to go. I was happy where I was. All my friends were there. I knew better than anyone what was good for me and what was going to make me happy, and this was definitely not it.

Finally my father said to me, "I'm asking you to do this because I believe it is the best thing for you. But I'll tell you what: you go there this fall, and if you're not happy at Christmas you can come back."

Armed with that ironclad escape clause, I reluctantly left for my new school that September.

Believe it or not, I had been there only a few days when it began to dawn on me that maybe this new school was not so bad after all. I made a lot of new friends. I saw opportunities to get involved in activities that were not available to me before. I began to see that I could actually be *happy* here.

My father could see it, too. Only a month or so had passed when he said to me, "I guess we don't need to wait until Christmas to see whether you're going to like it." And I said, "No, we don't."

What I learned in those few weeks was that what my father and mother had wanted me to do was far better than what I had wanted to do. They really did know better than I what was best for me.

Obedience Brings God's Blessings

I am still learning that lesson with my Father in heaven. What he wants me to do is always better than what I have in mind. My ideas, my ways, my plans are never as good as his. Sometimes I experience that same reluctance to give up my preferences and accept his. But when I do I remember my teenage experience and resolve once again to follow God's way and not my own. When I am obedient to God's word, I experience a rich and full life.

Paul, in his letter to the Galatians, expresses it like this: "The fruit of the Spirit is love, joy, peace, patience, kindness, goodness, faithfulness, gentleness, self-control" (Gal 5:22).

Obedience to God's word brings so many blessings. Haven't you found that to be true in your own life? Don't you want more of it?

The word of God has power to make a difference in our daily lives. Reading the Bible is not like reading a magazine or a newspaper or some other secular book. Scripture does not just give us interesting viewpoints or good advice or handy ideas. It gives us God's word. It helps us see with God's eyes, understand with his mind, love with his heart. It has power to change us, to make us more like the Lord himself. "For the word of God is living and active, sharper than any two-edged sword, piercing to the division of soul and spirit, of joints and marrow, and discerning the thoughts and intentions of the heart" (Heb 4:12).

Surely that is what we want more than anything: to be transformed into the image of Jesus. To enter into the love, joy, peace, patience, kindness, goodness, faithfulness, gentleness, and self-control that characterize Jesus and that are promised to us if we will be obedient to God and his word. The Lord tells us that if we abide in him, and if we allow his words to abide in us—in other words, if we are obedient—we can experience this kind of life here and now.

Obedience Brings Friendship with God

Obedience brings life; life now and life eternal; life in all its fullness and richness. Obedience also brings something more: it brings friendship with God. It opens to us the privilege of being numbered among his company.

"This is my commandment, that you love one another as I have loved you. Greater love has no man than this, that a man lay down his life for his friends. You are my friends if you do what I command you. No longer do I call you servants, for the servant does not know what his master is doing; but I have called you friends, for all that I have heard from my Father I have made known to you." (Jn 15:12-15)

Jesus here tells us quite plainly that he will set forth for us all that the Father has revealed to him, and that if we will obey his word we will be his friends. What a joy! What a privilege and honor to be called a friend of God, to be among those who live in intimate union with him.

You might think that my experiences in childhood and adolescence would have taught me once and for all about obedience. But I am afraid they did not, at least not completely. When I became an adult, I adopted an attitude that said, "I'm grown up now. I'm not a child, not a teenager any more. I'm an adult. I have to think for myself, make my own decisions, determine for myself what is best for me."

I am sure you can already see what was wrong with this line of thinking, but God had to teach it to me through a series of painful experiences. One experience in particular brought home to me the way that obedience can make us friends of God.

"Yes, But . . ."

For six years I had been living as part of a wonderful Christian community, the Servants of Christ the King, in Steubenville, Ohio. I loved it there. I loved the place, I loved the people, I loved the work God had given me to do.

So it came as something of a shock when the leaders of the community told me one day that they sensed the Lord calling me to spend some time in a different community, The Word of God, in Ann Arbor, Michigan. It was an older and more established community, they said; I would be able to learn a lot there. And it was the home of a publishing house that served Christians all over the world, they pointed out; I would have new and expanded opportunities to serve the Lord and his people.

I knew these leaders; I knew that they loved the Lord and that they loved me; I knew they were capable of hearing the Lord on my behalf. Besides, by now I was beginning to recognize a pattern: God breaking in just when I was feeling comfortable and calling me to something new. So I took this advice seriously. I prayed about it long and hard. And I heard the Lord speak to me and confirm the new direction.

In the face of all this, what was there left to say? I said yes. I told the Lord I would do what I knew he was calling me to do.

But there was one catch. I would *do* it, I decided, but I did not *like* it. I had to be obedient to God's call, but because that call frankly went against my personal preferences, I did not have to like it. My body would go to Ann Arbor, but not my heart.

Beyond Obedience

Apparently my approach manifested itself in my attitude and behavior. It was not long before a friend sat me down and gave me a good talking-to. Thank God he had provided me with friends who loved me too much to let me get away with this kind of mean-spirited response to the Lord!

"You know," she began, "It's really not enough for you to just do God's will."

"What do you mean?" I asked.

"You also have to *love* God's will," she said gently.

"Oh, come on," I replied. "What are you trying to do? Squeeze blood out of a stone? I know what God wants me to do, and I'm going to do it even though I don't want to. Isn't that enough?"

Her response represented a major turning point in my life.

"You believe God is a God of love, don't you? I mean, you speak and write about it all the time."

She had me there. "Yes," I said, "I believe God is a God of love."

"And you believe that God can only act out of love, don't you?"

"Well . . . yes," I said, wondering where this line of thinking was headed.

"Well, if God is a God of love, and if everything he calls you to do is an act of his perfect love for you, then how could you ever want anything but his will for your life? How could you *not* love it?"

I was starting to get fidgety.

"Your preferences certainly have a place in discerning God's will," she said, "but once you *know* what God's will is, you have to set your preferences aside and *embrace* his will, because you know it is his greatest act of love toward you. Why waste your energy resisting God? Close the door on your own preferences and embrace God's will. It will bring you life."

Closing the Door to Self

I had to take a very long walk after that conversation. But finally I wrestled my way to the place where I could accept the wise words my friend had spoken. "Okay, Lord," I said at last. "I'll do it, if you'll help me. I'll close the door on my preferences and I'll embrace your will."

The moment I made that decision I experienced the presence of God in a way I never had before. I experienced God so near to me. In my heart I heard him say, "I love you. If I could take you home with me now I would, but the Father has much for you to do." I experienced a fellowship, an intimacy with God that I had never known before.

Sometimes we face choices between something bad and something good, and those choices can be difficult enough. Other times—as in this case—we face choices between something good and something better, and those can be even harder. But when we do choose the better portion, not just out of dutiful compliance but with a heart to embrace God's loving will, we draw even closer to the heart of God. We experience the privilege, the honor, the joy of being near him—of being called his *friend.*

Three Questions to Check Our Obedience

So far I have been focusing on some of the benefits that come to us as a result of obeying God's word. But obedience puts us in position not just to receive benefits and blessings from the Lord, but also to effectively pray for benefits and blessings for others. Obedience enables us to hear God and then to orient our prayer according to *his will.*

That is what it means to pray "in his name": not just to add the words, "I ask it in your name, Lord," to the end of our prayer, but to *know* the mind and heart of God from his word, and thus to *know* that what we pray for corresponds with his will. We can then act as his representative and wield the power of prayer on his behalf, "in his name."

Intercession is a weapon of spiritual warfare. God wants us to be spiritual warriors who can take up that weapon and wield it on behalf of him and his kingdom. But the first requirement of any warrior is that he or she be obedient to the direction of the captain. The Lord Jesus is our captain in spiritual warfare. That is why it is so important that we be obedient to him and his word if we are to serve in his army.

Let me give you three questions that you can ask yourself to help you determine where you stand as regards obedience to the Lord and readiness to serve him in a life of intercessory prayer.

First, do I discipline myself to spend time each day reading, studying, meditating upon, and praying with Scripture? Is God's word becoming part of me? Is it being worked into the very fiber of my being?

Second, do I follow through and make concrete, practical decisions in order that God's word may be a living reality in my daily life?

It is so easy to become what James described as "hearers of the word but not doers of the word" (see Jas 1:22-25). We read the beautiful words of Scripture and we say, "Ah, yes. That's what I want to do. That's the kind of person I want to be. How wonderful." But then we leave our prayer time and fail to put those words into practice. As a result, nothing really changes; we may even frustrate ourselves by our failure to conform to what we have read.

The solution is simple (though sometimes painful in practice): at the end of each prayer time, ask the Lord, "What am I to do *today* to apply the lessons I have learned from your word?" Then do it!

Third, do I make myself accountable to someone for how well I am obeying God's word?

This is a tough one—but, as I have found in my own experience, an indispensable one. The sad fact is that I can make all kinds of wonderful promises to God, and then fail to follow through on them. It is only when I tell them to another person, and ask that person to pursue me as to how I am following through on them, that they really seem to have any teeth.

Naturally, I am careful to do this with someone who understands and shares my desire to grow in holiness, someone in whom I can freely confide what is going on in my life. It is not always easy—as with the friend who called me on regarding my decision to move to Ann Arbor. But it is a great blessing to know that there is someone who loves you enough to speak the truth to you when you need it most.

Answering these questions will help us assess our obedience and make our intercession more fruitful. It will draw us to commit ourselves to obey God's word: to study it so that we know what the will of God is, and to actively apply it to our own life situation.

His Word Is Written on Our Hearts

As we conclude this discussion, let's look once more at Deuteronomy chapter 30: the chapter in which God explains that obedience to his word is the key to entering into the life he has in store for us:

"For this commandment which I command you this day is not too hard for you, neither is it far off. It is not in heaven, that you should say, 'Who will go up for us to heaven, and bring it to us, that we may hear it and do it?' Neither is it beyond the sea, that you should say, 'Who will go over the sea for us, and bring it to us, that we may hear it and do it?' But the word is very near you; it is in your mouth and in your heart, so that you can do it." (Dt 30:11-14)

The word of God is clear, it is simple, it is readily available to us. God has come in the person of his Son Jesus to reveal it to us. He has caused it to be written down in the Bible for us, so that we can read it, study it, and meditate on it. He has caused it to be written upon our hearts and has given us the Holy Spirit to dwell inside us and to bring his word to life within us.

What Could Be Better Than Obedience?

So often we try to confuse and complicate matters. We need simply to realize that the word of God is near to us, and that all that remains is for us to carry it out:

"See, I have set before you this day life and good, death and evil. If you obey the commandments of the LORD your God which I command you this day, by loving the LORD your God, by walking in his ways, and by keeping his commandments and his statutes and his ordinances, then you shall live and multiply, and the LORD your God will bless you in the land which you are entering to take possession of it. But if your heart turns away, and you will not hear, but are drawn away to worship other gods and serve them, I declare

to you this day, that you shall perish; you shall not live long in the land which you are going over the Jordan to enter and possess.
I call heaven and earth to witness against you this day, that I have set before you life and death, blessing and curse; therefore choose life, that you and your descendants may live, loving the LORD your God, obeying his voice, and cleaving to him; for that means life to you." (Dt 30:15-20)

The Lord offers us life, riches, and blessing. He offers us the incomprehensible privilege of being his friend. He offers the assurance that our prayers will be heard. All in return for obedience to his word. What else could we desire? What else could we ever wish to choose? Let us make the decisions in our lives that we need to make in order that God's word may abide in us and that we may follow after him in all things, thus experiencing the abundant provision that he has for us.

Part III

A Life of Faithfulness

Standing Our Ground

WE HAVE SPOKEN OF BEING CALLED to live a life of love: a life of experiencing the love God has for us and of passing that love on to others. And we have spoken of being called to live a life of prayer: a life of fellowship and intimacy with God for our own sake and a life of fruitful intercessory prayer for the sake of others. Now we must speak of another aspect to our lives, one that solidifies the other two and multiplies their effectiveness many times over: living a life of *faithfulness*.

I like to think of faithfulness as the quality of *standing firm*, as Paul described it in his letter to the Ephesians:

> Finally, be strong in the Lord and in the strength of his might. Put on the whole armor of God, that you may be able to *stand* against the wiles of the devil.... Therefore take the whole armor of God, that you may be able to withstand in the evil day, and having done all, to *stand. Stand* therefore.... (Eph 6:10-11, 13-14)

I have often pondered these verses, especially the fact that Paul uses the word *stand* so many times. I think he is saying something very important to us. I think he is saying that one of the most crucial things we can do in living for and serving the Lord is simply to stand firm in the place where God has put us. To hold fast to what he has taught us. To hang on to every inch of territory he has helped us to take in our struggle to live a life worthy of his kingdom. Not to pull back. Not to retreat. Not to give up. Not to become discouraged in the face of difficulties, but to stand firm.

What does it mean to "stand firm?" It means to dig our heels in. To be rooted. To be unmovable. To be unshakable. To let nothing move us from the position God has placed us in. To let go of nothing he has taught us. To let nothing turn us back from following after him, come what may. To hold our ground, regardless of what the world, the flesh, or the devil may throw at us.

Bearing Love, Bearing Life

Not surprisingly, two of the places where I think the Lord most wants us to stand firm are the two we have already discussed: love and prayer.

Surely if there is one thing that God wants each of us to be as his sons and daughters, it is to be channels of his love. God *is* love, and wherever God's people are, there God's love should be manifest.

Let me emphasize the *wherever*: we are to be channels of God's love every place we are. At home. At school. At the office. On the job site. Into every situation we are part of, we are to bring kindness, mercy, compassion, and forgiveness. We bring truth—in love. We bring discipline—in love. We bring strength—in love. We bring *life*, because we bring the life-giving love of God.

Standing Firm against the Flesh

There is something in us that wars against this. Scripture calls it "the flesh." This refers not to our actual skin-and-bones flesh, but to that part of us that still craves its own comfort, its own satisfaction, its own way. In one place Paul refers to it as "the old man" who still lives on, even within the new creation that we have become in Christ.

Make no mistake about it, the flesh is real. And it stands utterly opposed to what God wants to do in us and through us:

> Walk by the Spirit, and do not gratify the desires of the flesh. For the desires of the flesh are against the Spirit, and the desires of the Spirit are against the flesh; for these are opposed to each other, to prevent you from doing what you would. (Gal 5:16-17)

To drive home the point that the flesh is not to be taken lightly, Paul enumerates some of its characteristics:

> Now the works of the flesh are plain: fornication, impurity, licentiousness, idolatry, sorcery, enmity, strife, jealousy, anger, selfishness, dissension, party spirit, envy, drunkenness, carousing, and the like. I warn you, as I warned you before, that those who do such things shall not inherit the kingdom of God. (Gal 5:19-21)

Strong words! But important words, because they show how our flesh wars against love. Indeed, it wars against life itself, and seeks only to deal us death. How many times, in large ways and small, does our flesh rise up and try to deflect us from bringing life and love into the situations we are part of?

Surely here is a place where Paul's exhortation to stand firm applies. We must stand against the flesh, and we must stand firm for love. This means consciously and aggressively choosing *against* death and *for* life, *against* the works of the flesh and *for* what Paul later calls "the fruit of the Spirit"—the first quality of which is love.

Standing Firm against Discontent

Not only the flesh, but Satan himself wars against a life of love. He who is the great dealer of death and hatred seeks to choke off life and love wherever he can. How does he do it? He undermines our confidence in our standing as children of God. He drags up our sins and weaknesses and flings them accusingly in our faces. He stirs up wrong attitudes and motives. He tells us lies.

Sometimes his work is quite apparent. But most of the time it is extremely subtle, requiring careful discernment. For example, one of the ways I believe the evil one wars against our living a life of love is by fostering dissatisfaction and discontent. No doubt you have heard someone—perhaps yourself!—say things like these:

"I don't have a husband and I wish I did."

"I do have a husband and I wish I had a different one."

"I wish I had a job."

"I wish I had any job but this one."

"I wish I had more children."

"I wish I had fewer children."

"I wish I had any other children but these."

"I wish I had a house."

"I wish this house could be different."

And so it goes, on and on. Discontented. Finding fault. Never satisfied. Grumbling and complaining before the Lord, who made us who we are and placed us where we are out of love! Do you see why Satan wants to draw us into this trap? Because it causes us to turn away from the love of God as it is expressed in the provision God has made for our lives.

We cannot stand firm when we are indulging discontent. When we are giving free reign to discontent, we are always looking to the right or to the left, never straight ahead on the plan God has for our life. How can we stand our ground against the enemy if our eyes are not on the Lord who alone can give us the strength to conquer?

Choosing to Love

A very dear friend of mine lost her teenage son to cancer a few years ago. Just before the funeral, she and her husband were dismayed to learn that the husband also had cancer. In the years since then, he has had to undergo several operations. All this has resulted in a severe strain on their family (they have seven other children) and on their finances.

I will never forget going to visit them at the time of their son's funeral. I was staying in an upstairs guest room. Early in the morning of the funeral, my friend came into my room with a cup of tea, just to chat, to find out how I was doing, to talk with me about the Lord. *She* brought *me* refreshment! She brought me life, even at the moment of her greatest grief.

Does she know pain? Does she weep? Does she cry out to God and ask, "Why is this happening to me?" Of course she does. She is close enough to the Lord to be real with him. But she also stands her ground. Never have I been with her but she gives of herself to refresh me and bless me and impart life to me. She stands firm, living a life of love.

Does she have to work to put to death the works of the flesh? Does she fail and need to repent? Of course she does. She is human. But she is also determined to live by the Spirit and not gratify the desires of the flesh. She chooses to love and to share the life of God with others. And God honors her choice.

The First Corinthians Standard

I would like to suggest a simple tool that can help us evaluate how well we are doing at living a life of love and can show us where we still need to learn to stand our ground.

The tool is the very familiar passage about love: chapter 13 of the first letter of Paul to the Corinthians. We have all heard it many times, and we may even know it by heart. I would like to focus on verses four to seven, in which Paul gives his definition of love. But I would like to suggest a slightly modified version of this passage. I suggest that you read through it, and in every place where it offers a description of what love is, put your name instead. In the original form the passage reads like this:

Love is patient and kind; love is not jealous or boastful; it is not arrogant or rude. Love does not insist on its own way; it is not irritable or resentful; it does not rejoice at wrong, but rejoices in the right. Love bears all things, believes all things, hopes all things, endures all things.

In our revised form, using myself as an example, it would read like this:

Ann is patient and kind; Ann is not jealous or boastful; she is not arrogant or rude. Ann does not insist on her own way; she is not irritable or resentful; she does not rejoice at wrong, but rejoices in the right. Ann bears all things, believes all things, hopes all things, endures all things.

Try it for yourself. Insert your own name and see how the passage reads. Does it give an accurate representation of you? Or does it point to areas where you need more of God's grace to stand your ground in living a life of love?

None of us is perfect. None of us can live a life of love on our own. All of us will fail from time to time. I may finish writing this chapter and half an hour later find myself getting impatient with someone! Then what? Do I grow discouraged? No. I simply acknowledge my failing to the Lord, ask for his help, seek forgiveness from the person I have wounded, and resolve to choose for love more vigorously the next time I am tempted to irritability. All of us need more of God's grace to grow in a life of love. But God is ready to give us that grace when we seek it!

Standing Firm in Prayer

The second area we have discussed, and in which we need to stand firm, is intercession. Paul specifically mentions this later in the same passage we have been examining, the one where he calls us to "stand": "Pray at all times in the Spirit, with all prayer and supplication. To that end keep alert with all perseverance, making supplication for all the saints" (Eph 6:18).

I think it is clear from the context of this passage that no one is excluded from the call to vigorous, faithful intercessory prayer. We all must pray. Certainly some of us will experience a special call, a special gift, a special anointing, for intercession. But all of us, because we are Christians, are in some way and to some degree called to be intercessors.

Intercession: A Weapon of Spiritual Warfare

We are in a war, and intercessory prayer is one of the major weapons God has given us for fighting that war. Satan is trying to win the hearts, minds, and souls of men and women all over the world. He wants to draw as many of them into hell as he possibly can. I believe God has given us intercessory prayer as a means for us to fight with him and draw many into heaven. God honors our prayer. He uses it to revive his people and he uses it to call men and women to himself. He wants us to take up intercessory prayer as a warrior would take up a sword, and go into battle at his side.

Two things happen when we pray. The first is that God changes people and situations around us. He touches hearts. He rearranges circumstances. He redirects attitudes and behavior. This, of course, is what we think of first when we think of intercession: God changing others.

But God also changes *us*. That is the second thing that happens when we pray. He touches *our* hearts. He rearranges *our* circumstances. He redirects *our* attitudes and behavior. We become more purified as vessels of his love, his grace, his power. We become better able to hear his voice and carry out his will. We become more useful to him as servants.

"Beloved," wrote Peter to the early Christians, "do not be surprised at the fiery ordeal which comes upon you to prove you, as though something strange were happening to you. But rejoice in so far as you share Christ's sufferings, that you may also rejoice and be glad when his glory is revealed" (1 Pt 4:12-13).

Peter was not speaking here specifically of intercession, but there is no doubt that when we take up the weapon of intercessory prayer and go into battle, the fighting often gets more intense. We should not be surprised or caught off guard by this. It is not uncommon that we pray for a difficult situation only to see it get worse for a time! Then we are tempted to think, "Great. I prayed, and look what happened. I made it worse. I must be a pretty miserable intercessor."

Don't listen to that lie. When the battle heats up, it is usually a sign that our prayers are beginning to have an effect: it tells us that Satan has felt the sting of our prayer and is fighting back. Stand your ground. Dig in your heels and resolve that you are not going to back off. Ask God to sustain you and to show you again and again specifically how to pray. But don't give in. Stand firm.

A Ten-Year Struggle

In chapter six I described how the Lord has led me to pray for family members and other loved ones based on Matthew 6:33. Discovering that principle was the culmination of a lengthy process of "standing firm" in prayer for a particular member of my own family. He had long been in difficulty, and I was praying that God would touch his life. I could see so many circumstances in his life and in the family situation that seemed to be lined up against this ever happening. It was in 1976 that I started to pray, and I prayed faithfully for it in every way I could think of for more than ten years.

It was in April 1985 that God finally taught me to intercede in terms of repentance, faith, and life in the Spirit rather than in terms of the myriad circumstances that had so overwhelmed his life. Do you know what happened? Less than a year after I and others began to pray in this way, he gave his life to the Lord!

God used that long period of time to teach me what it means to stand firm in prayer. He also adjusted my prayer as I went along, helping me conform it more and more to his will. I am still praying, because I believe there is more that God wants to do in this person's life. But I am more confident than ever that I am on the right track and that I must continue to stand my ground.

"I Wonder Who Has Been Praying?"

Recently a woman who had heard me speak on this topic wrote to me to tell me of an answered prayer in her own family. "For years," she said, "I prayed for my father. He was an alcoholic and had been extremely difficult to get along with. Family life was very, very hard. I prayed that his many weaknesses would be healed. I prayed that his disruptive behavior would change. I prayed that the effects of his disruptive behavior would somehow be lessened.

"Then I heard you talk about interceding that our loved ones repent and come to know the Lord, and I began to pray that way for my father. It was only a few weeks later that he gave his life to Jesus. I could hardly believe it! He became a different person. He became a source of joy and delight. The family was brought together in a way it had not been in years.

"I am writing now to tell you that three weeks after my father gave his life to the Lord, he died. We are sad, but we are also very happy because the most important thing of all happened for him, and because we had the chance to rejoice in it together before he died. We know that one day we will all be together again."

A friend of mine recently said something that really struck a chord with me. "Whenever I see something good happen," he said, "I think to myself, 'I wonder who has been praying?'"

God answers the prayer of those who do not give up. Those who stand firm. Even if we find ourselves praying for many years, we can know that God is honoring our faithfulness, and that he will continue to adjust us and guide us in our praying.

Stand, Therefore

Brothers and sisters, we are in a battle. The Lord has called us to fight at his side for the sake of his kingdom. He wants us to be men and women who love: who inject his life into every situation we are part of. He wants us to be men and women who pray: who wield the weapon of intercessory prayer in order that his kingdom may be established in those around us.

"Stand, therefore," says Paul. Stand firm in living a life of love. Stand firm in living a life of prayer. For it is through lives of love and prayer, lived in faithfulness, that God will change the world.

TEN

The Eternal Perspective

S OMETIMES SPIRITUAL BREAKTHROUGHS HAPPEN in the strangest places. Like the coffee shop where I got my first real glimpse of heaven.

There were six of us going out for breakfast on a weekday morning. No big deal. Just a group of friends planning to spend some time together, to talk about how things had been going lately, to try and encourage one another in our walk with the Lord.

We had just finished placing our orders when, for no particular reason, we got to talking about what it would be like to be in heaven. What would it be like to be somewhere where all sadness was banished and where joy reigned? What would it be like to live where there was no dissension, no friction, nothing but peace?

The more we got into it, the more excited we became. What would it be like to live where all hope was fully realized? Where everything our spirits had ever longed for was perfectly fulfilled? Where there was no discouragement, no sadness, no despair, no oppression, no depression? What would it be like to be where all darkness was banished? To see nothing but fullness of light and life in every situation?

Someone remembered the passage from the New Testament where Paul says that in heaven God will be everything to everyone (1 Cor 15:28). What does that mean, we wondered? What would it be like to have God himself be the direct, unmediated, all-sufficient source of everything we can even conceive of desiring?

Most of all: what would it be like to see God face to face? To actually *see* him? No longer "through a glass, darkly," but clearly and plainly and without distortion? In the Old Testament it was held that if you so much as caught a glimpse of the face of God, even for a split second, even by accident, you would die. It was that overpowering an experience. What would it be like to *gaze* upon the face of God for all eternity?

A Fleeting Taste of Heaven

I said there were six of us at the table that morning, but of course that is not quite accurate. Looking back on it, I can see that the Lord himself was there with us as well. No doubt you have had a similar experience at some time in your life. Seemingly mundane, routine surroundings are transformed by what can only be called a visitation of the Holy Spirit, and your life is changed forever after.

That innocent-looking breakfast gathering was such an experience for me. It changed my life. Something deep inside me was touched, like a long-dormant ember being fanned into flame. Suddenly I understood what I had read so many times in the writings of holy men and women: that heaven is the heart's deepest longing, that all our other desires are but pale reflections of it.

That morning, for the first time, I knew what it meant to *want* to go to heaven, to *want* to see God. Not just because I had been taught as a child that I was supposed to want it. No, but because I had caught sight of it, just for a moment; I had tasted it ever so fleetingly on my tongue and knew I could never be satisfied until I fully possessed it and was fully possessed by it.

A Higher Reality

Certainly you know as well as I how easy it is for us to be weighed down by the cares and concerns of this life. Day-to-day circumstances, details and difficulties, the nitty-gritty hardships, trials, temptations, and sins. There is an almost overwhelming tendency for us to focus all our attention on these things, and then on ourselves and how well or poorly we are dealing with them.

That breakfast-table conversation reminded me that there is so much more to life than what I see and taste and touch all around me day in and day out. There is a whole other dimension of reality above the dimension of earthly life. Keeping that spiritual dimension of reality in mind gives me an entirely different perspective on the earthly dimension. It puts everything—all the trials and tribulations and circumstances and situations—in a completely different context.

I walked out of that coffee shop a different person from when I had walked in. The other women said the same thing. They said, "We've got to do this again some time. We've got to talk some more about heaven. It's given me a new perspective. It's given me courage. It's given me a lightness of heart. It's helped me understand what I'm here for, why I'm doing the things I'm doing, where it's all headed."

The View from the Mountaintop

This is what I call having an "eternal perspective"—seeing our lives not from the limited vantage point of our own earthly, human experience, but from the vantage point of heaven. It is like the difference between standing in the bottom of the valley and standing at the top of the mountain.

There is an old saying that says, "Some people are so heavenly-minded that they're no earthly good." That is not what I am talking about. I am not talking about getting so focused on the afterlife that we withdraw from this life. I am not talking about living so much in the "then and there" that we become absent from the here and now. God placed us in the here and now, and that is where he wants us to dwell, to be bearers of his light, life, and truth.

But it is equally true that as we live our lives in the here and now, we must have our sights set on the right things. We must know *why* we are doing what we are doing, where it is all headed, what is the point of it all. And the point of it all is heaven; life with God in the fullness of his kingdom; eternal righteousness, peace, and joy. The only worthwhile goal in life is to get to heaven ourselves and to take as many people with us as we can. Keeping our eyes on the goal and living our lives in the meantime with it in view is what it means to keep an eternal perspective.

Seek the Things that Are Above

After that breakfast conversation I began to ask myself, how do I foster this eternal perspective? How do I keep it alive? It was as though I were looking back on the whole experience and saying, That was a wonderful place to visit, but how can I *live* there?

When I asked the Lord about this in prayer, the first thing he did was direct me to some passages from Scripture. I made them the subject of my meditation in the ensuing weeks; I encourage you to become familiar with them and to meditate on them as well (you might want to turn back to chapter 5 for a quick review on how to meditate on Scripture).

The first passage the Lord led me to was from Paul's letter to the Colossians:

> If then you have been raised with Christ, seek the things that are above, where Christ is, seated at the right hand of God. Set your minds on things that are above, not on things that are on earth. For you have died, and your life is hid with Christ in God. When Christ who is our life appears, then you also will appear with him in glory. (Col 3:1-4)

What a magnificent statement of the eternal perspective! We *have died*, Paul says, we *have been* raised with Christ. It is an accomplished fact. As a result, our lives are now "hid with

Christ in God." In a real sense, our lives are no longer "here and now." Therefore it is short-sighted and counterproductive to focus our energies on "things that are on earth." The logical thing, the necessary thing, is to set our minds "on the things that are above, where Christ is," and where our lives really are as well.

Rooted in Eternity

Paul gives a similar exhortation, in somewhat different terms, in his letter to the Romans:

> I appeal to you therefore, brethren, by the mercies of God, to present your bodies as a living sacrifice, holy and acceptable to God, which is your spiritual worship. Do not be conformed to this world but be transformed by the renewal of your mind, that you may prove what is the will of God, what is good and acceptable and perfect. (Rom 12:1-2)

Both this passage and the one from Colossians speak about our minds. They call us to get our minds rooted in eternal truths, not merely in mundane, present-day realities. We must live out our lives amid those realities, it is true. But where are our roots? It is only as we are rooted in the eternal realities that we will have the wisdom and strength we need to deal with the present realities.

The Hope of Salvation

This emphasis on "the mind" recalled another passage that has to do with maintaining an eternal perspective, from the passage of Paul's letter to the Ephesians that deals with spiritual warfare, the passage we looked at in the previous chapter. One line in particular is appropriate for our present discussion: "Take the helmet of salvation" (Eph 6:17).

The helmet, obviously, is the piece of protective armor worn on the head. In spiritual terms, this relates to safeguarding our minds. One of the ways we guard our minds, keep them properly focused, is by putting on the helmet of salvation.

Very well, you say; but what does that *mean?* Paul explains it in his first letter to the Thessalonians, where he urges us to "put on the breastplate of faith and love, *and for a helmet the hope of salvation*" (1 Thes 5:8). The "helmet" is the hope of salvation: confident expectation that God will do what he has promised to do, that everything will be as he has said it would.

To say that we have hope in salvation does not mean that we simply wish it were for real: "Gee, I hope there's a heaven but I really don't know . . ." No, it means to hold before our eyes the reality of what Jesus accomplished on the cross: that he died for our sins and was raised to life again to open the way to heaven for us; that we are destined for heaven if we faithfully follow the Lord.

We are confident that God is there, that he will act on our behalf. We know that no matter what the battle is or how fiercely it rages, God will be triumphant. To wear the helmet of salvation into battle is to cling to the confident assurance that God is there and he is for us. It is to maintain the eternal perspective.

His Grace Is There to Help Us

One of the most important things for us to remember when we read Scripture is that God gives us the grace and power to do everything that he calls us to do. If he tells us to do something in his word, then we can know for sure that he will give us what we need to do it.

We need to be clear that all this applies to *us*. So often we read Scripture and we make all kinds of excuses for why the call does not apply to us or or why the promises do not apply to us and so on. But Scripture is not written just for "everyone else." It is written every bit as much for you and for me. The call to live a life of love, the call to live a life of prayer, the call to live a life of faithfulness, the call to maintain an eternal perspective—all these calls extend to you and me. What is more, the promise that God will give us the things we need to *answer* his call also extends to you and to me.

Scripture tells us to seek the things that are above. It tells us not to set our minds on the things of earth. It tells us to let ourselves be transformed by the renewing of our mind. It tells us to wear the helmet of hope, of our salvation. If Scripture tells us all these things, then we can know for certain that the grace of God and the power of the Holy Spirit will be available to help us do it.

It is crucial that we grasp this right from the outset. It is not just that living our earthly life with an eternal perspective would be nice, if only it were possible. It is that such a way of living *is* possible, and is possible for you and for me. It does not matter who we are, where we have been, or what our circumstances are. God's word is true, and God's power is there to back it up. If we turn to him and tell him that our desire is to live this way, he will help us do it.

Where Is Home Base?

When I first began purposefully to pursue living with an eternal perspective, I had to remind myself of these truths many times: *God calls me to set my mind on the things that are above, where Christ is. God's word is true. God's grace is here to help me. O Lord, work in my life. Help me set my mind on you. Accomplish your purpose in me.*

After I had spent some time simply getting these truths embedded in my mind and heart, I sensed the Lord giving me some questions to reflect on regarding my life. They are questions that I believe can be helpful to all of us as we seek to be transformed by the renewal of our minds and to live with our minds set on the things that are above.

The first question was what might be called diagnostic: it was designed to help me get clear about where my thoughts and energies were actually being invested. The Lord said, "What do you think about when your mind is not directly occupied with some task?"

"Well," I thought, "I think about lots of things. I think about what's on my schedule for the rest of the day, I think about what I'm planning to do tomorrow, I go over conversations I've had with people, I think about conversations I'm going to have with people, I think about how I'm going to handle this or that problem...." It was not long until I realized that my mind certainly is not set on the things that are above very much of the time.

Now obviously there *is* a place for thinking about the ins and outs of daily life. But the point of the question the Lord asked me was, I believe, "Where does your mind naturally gravitate when it is *not* of necessity focused on some present concern? Where is 'home base?'"

Our Mind Must Be Disciplined

I was not quite satisfied with my mind's "home base." How was I to change it? The first step the Lord led me to was memorizing the very Scripture passages that had launched the whole series of reflections in the first place, the ones we have looked at already in this chapter. The second step was cutting back on some of the other things with which, I came to realize, I had too often filled my mind in the past: things like television, magazines, other forms of entertainment.

After that came disciplining myself not to hang on to anxious or angry thoughts. They pop into my mind from time to time just as they do into everyone's, but I learned I did not need to dwell on them. Instead, I could replace them with more worthwhile thoughts, such as the ones that flowed from the Scripture passages I had learned. The whole exercise was reminiscent of the poetic passage that concludes the core of Paul's letter to the Philippians:

Finally, brethren, whatever is true, whatever is honorable, whatever is just, whatever is pure, whatever is lovely, whatever is gracious, if there is any excellence, if there is anything worthy of praise, think about these things. What you have learned and received and heard and seen in me, do; and the God of peace will be with you. (Phil 4:8-9)

Keeping Our Eyes on Heaven

Then the Lord posed a series of questions that had to do with the goal, the purpose, the central organizing principle, of my life. He asked me—and I think he asks all of us—"How much do you think and live and act in terms of the age to come? Do you work simply to enjoy good things in this world, or do you use them to serve the life to come? Are you raising your children to succeed in this life only, or are you raising them for the life to come? What about your career? Do you use your talents simply to get ahead in this world, or do you orient them to the life to come? You can have all these things, and use them and enjoy them, in this life. But your main focus should always be on the life to come."

A Woman of Valor

Finally, by way of teaching me how to live with an eternal perspective, I felt led to read the lives of some holy men and women from the very earliest days of Christianity. Most of them lived in situations in which being a follower of Christ was not accepted; as a result they ultimately became martyrs. In their lives, I sensed the Lord telling me, I would find models for living with my mind set on the things above.

The most moving story I read had to do with a woman

known to history as Saint Crispina, who lived in the part of North Africa where the great Augustine would one day be bishop. She died in the year A.D. 304.

Crispina was a woman of noble birth. She was wealthy, both by virtue of her own family's fortune and by virtue of having married into wealth. She was the mother of several children. She was also a firm Christian, living in the midst of a time of terrible persecution.

The day came when she was arrested by order of the pro-consul and brought before his tribunal. He asked her if she was aware of the imperial edict that commanded all persons to sacrifice to the gods of the empire.

"I never sacrifice, nor will I sacrifice, to any other than to the one God and to our Lord Jesus Christ, his Son, who was born and suffered for us," replied Crispina.

The pro-consul replied, "Abandon your foolish superstition and adore the gods."

"Every day," she answered, "I adore my God. Beside him I recognize no other."

"Then I have no choice," said the pro-consul, "but to conclude that you are stubborn and that you hold the gods in contempt. You must therefore be made to experience the full rigor of the punishment set down in law."

She replied, "I shall most willingly suffer whatever may be exacted, as the testimony of my faith."

The pro-consul began to plead with her to save herself from death: "You shall lose your head unless you observe the commands of the emperor."

"God Is with Me"

But Crispina held firm. "No one," she said, "shall oblige me to sacrifice to demons. I sacrifice to the Lord and to him only, who made the heavens and the earth. I do not fear the anger of men. I fear only God who is in heaven."

Losing his patience, the pro-consul snapped, "Obey or your head shall be struck off at once."

Crispina replied evenly, "Then I shall return thanks to my Lord for considering me worthy of martyrdom. God is with me to strengthen me, that I may not consent to your commands."

It was on the fifth day of December, in the year 304, that Crispina gave the ultimate witness of faith and became a martyr for our Lord Jesus Christ.

Will God ever ask you or me to give that same witness? We do not know. If he does, will we be ready? Will we be clear about what is of greatest importance in our life? Will our mind have been set on the things that are above, where our life truly is hid with Christ in God?

I close this book with the story of Crispina because she seems to me to embody all that we have been talking about.* A life of love. A life of prayer. A life of faithfulness. A life lived in the light of eternity. A life thoroughly and completely given over to God.

May God grant to all of us the grace to live that kind of life.

*Excerpt from *Victories of the Martyrs,* Saint Alphonsus Liguori, (New York: Redemptorist Fathers, 1954; Reprinted Tan Publishers), pp. 106-8.

Other Books of Interest
from Servant Publications

Yielding to the Power of God
The Importance of Surrender, Abandonment,
and Obedience to God's Will
Ann Shields

Ann Shields reminds us of God's intimate and personal love
for each of us; she challenges us to surrender all doubt of
that. The reward for doing so will be greater holiness, joy, and
power than we have yet known. *$2.25*

Called to Holiness
What It Means to Encounter the Living God
Ralph Martin

Offers inspiration and practical help for Christians who
desire to grow in holiness. Ralph Martin describes the
consuming fire of God's holiness and explains how human
beings are designed to be holy. *$6.95*

Meeting God in Every Moment
The Art of Living in God's Presence
David E. Rosage

Experience God's powerful presence in the midst of every-
day life. Through fifty-two meditations, one for each week of
the year, Rosage helps us to see and hear, to know and love
God wherever we are, whatever we are doing. *$3.95*